Table of Contents

Practice Test #1

Practice Questions

1. Which of the following is usually the first form of study in a new area of scientific inquiry?
   - a. descriptive studies
   - b. controlled experiments
   - c. comparative data analysis
   - d. choosing a method and design

2. What is the purpose of conducting an experiment?
   - a. to test a hypothesis
   - b. to collect data
   - c. to identify a control state
   - d. to choose variables

3. Which unit represents 1/1000 of the basic metric unit of volume?
   - a. milliliter
   - b. centigram
   - c. kilogallon
   - d. deciquart

4. Which of the following measurements is equal to 25.4 centimeters?
   - a. 10 inches
   - b. 2.1 feet
   - c. 2.54 meters
   - d. 2540 millimeters

5. What laboratory practice can increase the accuracy of a measurement?
   - a. repeating the measurement several times
   - b. calibrating the equipment each time you use it
   - c. using metric measuring devices
   - d. following MSDS information

6. Which of the following is an example of a descriptive study?
   - a. correlational studies of populations
   - b. identifying a control
   - c. statistical data analysis
   - d. identifying dependent and independent variables

7. The diagram below shows a force *F* pulling a box up a ramp against the force of friction and the force of gravity. Which of the following diagrams correctly includes vectors representing the normal force, the force of gravity and the force of friction?

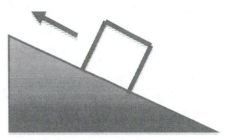

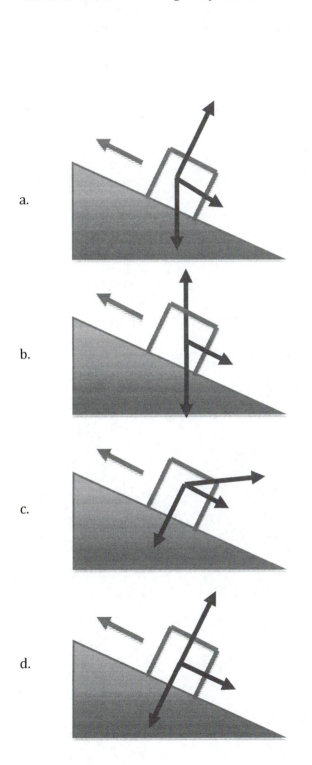

a.

b.

c.

d.

Question 8: Consider the following information in answering the question which follows:

> A class exercise involves demonstration of the principle of neutralization of acids and bases. The reagents available are 1 M NaOH, concentrated HCl, water, and phenol red [a pH indicator that turns from yellow to red under basic conditions]. The procedure chosen by the teacher is as follows:
>
> *Step 1*: Prior to class, the teacher prepares 1 M HCl by adding 914 ml water to 86 ml of HCl. [Note that concentrated HCl is 11.65 M.]
>
> *Step 2*: Since the class is divided into nine groups of three students, the teacher distributes the 1 M HCl into nine 125 ml flasks.
>
> *Step 3*: Each group is given a dropper bottle with phenol red, a bottle containing 200 ml of 1 M NaOH, and a 25 ml pipette with bulb.
>
> *Step 4*: The students are instructed to add the phenol red to the HCl until a visible yellow color is seen, record the color, then slowly add NaOH, and record the volume of NaOH required to make the solution alkaline.

8. What did the teacher do wrong in step 1?
   a. The volumes of acid and water are not additive. He/she should have added 500 ml of water and then after the mixture cooled brought the volume to exactly 1000 ml.
   b. HCl is a weak acid. He/she should have used more HCl to create a solution that is 1 M in hydronium ions.
   c. He/she should have added the acid to about 500 ml of water then brought the volume to exactly 1000 ml.
   d. He/she should have chilled the water used to reduce the heat of mixing.

9. How can a computer aided design (CAD) program be used in the laboratory setting?
   a. to collect and analyze digital data
   b. to write up a lab report
   c. to design a set of lab instructions
   d. to generate graphical models

10. Which of the following laboratory safety devices is recommended but not required by state law?
   a. containers for broken glassware
   b. eye protection for every student
   c. emergency showers
   d. fire blankets

11. Which of these signs shows the information contained on the Material Safety Data Sheet (MSDS)?

a.

b.

c.

d.

12. Which set of scientific thinkers are related to the study of chemistry?
    a. Newton, Einstein, Feinman, and Hawking
    b. Hooke, Pasteur, Watson & Crick, and Jacob & Monod
    c. Ibn Hayyan, Lavoisier, Mendeleev, and Curie
    d. Hutton, Darwin, Cuvier, and Wegener

13. The primary substances of which all other things are composed are
    a. compounds.
    b. electrons.
    c. molecules.
    d. elements.

14. The element in this list with chemical properties similar to magnesium is
    a. carbon.
    b. strontium.
    c. chlorine.
    d. boron.

15. The center of an atom is called the _____. It is composed of _____.
    a. nucleus; protons and neutrons.
    b. nucleus; protons and electrons.
    c. electron cloud; electrons and protons.
    d. electron cloud; electrons and neutrons.

16. Isotopes are two atoms of the same element that have different ____. They have the same number of ____, but a different number of ____.
   a. mass; protons; neutrons.
   b. ionization number; protons; electrons.
   c. charge; protons; electrons.
   d. mass; protons; electrons.

17. What is the electron configuration for an atom of nitrogen?
   a. $1s^2 2s^2 2p^3$
   b. $1K2 2L5$
   c. nucleus7p+7n, electron cloud7e-
   d. $1s^2 2p^5$

Use the information below to answer question 18:

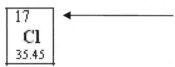

18. What information about the atom does the arrow point to?
   a. the atomic number or the number of protons
   b. the average atomic mass in atomic mass units
   c. the density of the element in g/mL
   d. the number of stable isotopes of the element

19. Which of the following would have the *most* massive radioactive decay?
   a. an alpha particle
   b. a beta ray
   c. gamma rays
   d. x-rays

20. Which of the following equations shows what happens when lead-210 decays through beta emission?
   a. $^{210}_{82}Pb \rightarrow e^- + ^{210}_{83}Bi$

   b. $^{210}_{82}Pb \rightarrow e^- + ^{210}_{83}Pb$

   c. $^{210}_{82}Pb \rightarrow ^{4}_{2}He + ^{214}_{84}Po$

   d. $^{210}_{82}Pb \rightarrow ^{4}_{2}He + ^{206}_{80}Po$

21. Radon-222 is a radioactive gas. It has a half-life of 3.82 days. How much of a 1g sample of Radon-222 remains after 38.2 days?
   a. 1/1024 of a gram
   b. 1/38.2 of a gram
   c. 1/10 of a gram
   d. 1/3.82 of a gram

22. How many calories of heat are absorbed by 100g of water as it heats up from 50°C to 55°C?
    a. 5 calories
    b. 50 calories
    c. 500 calories
    d. 550 calories

23. A 20 in tin rod is heated from 25°C to 75°C. Which equation could be used to correctly calculate the expansion of the rod?
    a. $(2.3 \times 10^{-5})(20)(75 - 25)$
    b. $(6.9 \times 10^{-5})(20)(75 - 25)$
    c. $(20)^3(2.54)^3(2.5)(75 - 25)$
    d. $(20)^3(2.54)^3(75 - 25)(K + 273)$

24. Any given temperature can be represented using three different temperature scales. Which temperature scale below yields a sequence of numbers from *lowest to highest* for the temperature of boiling water?
    a. °C, °F, K
    b. °F, °C, K
    c. °F, K, °C
    d. K, °C, °F

25. The boiling of water is an example of ____:
    a. a physical change.
    b. a chemical change.
    c. sublimation.
    d. condensation.

26. Which group of elements has a stable electron configuration?

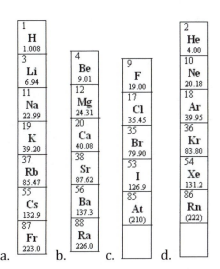

a.   b.   c.   d.

27. What change occurs when energy is added to a liquid?
    a. a phase change
    b. a chemical change
    c. sublimation
    d. condensation

28. Which group of elements is highly reactive, needs only one electron to fill their outer shells, and is known as the halogens?

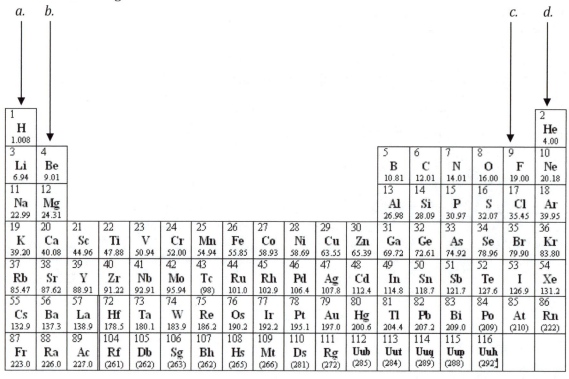

29. What happens to gas particles as temperature increases?
 a. The average kinetic energy decreases while the intermolecular forces increase.
 b. The average kinetic energy increases while the intermolecular forces decrease.
 c. Both the average kinetic energy and the intermolecular forces decrease.
 d. Both the average kinetic energy and the intermolecular forces increase.

30. A sample of gas occupies 22.4 L at 10°C and 1 atm. What is the new volume of the gas if the temperature increases to 100°C and the pressure increases to 2 atm?
 a. 8.97×10^{-4} L
 b. 8.93×10^{-3} L
 c. 7.51×10^{0} L
 d. 1.67×10^{1} L

31. What is the chemical formula for a compound that forms when sodium ions interact with phosphate ions?
 a. $NaPO$
 b. $NaPHO$
 c. $NaPO_4$
 d. Na_3PO_4

32. What is the chemical formula for aluminum sulfate?
   a. AlS
   b. $AlSO_4$
   c. $Al_2(SO_4)_3$
   d. $2Al_3SO_4$

33. Which of the following ratios shows a balanced chemical equation for:
$P_4 + O_2 \rightarrow P_2O_5$?
   a. $1\ P_4 + 1\ O_2 \rightarrow 1P_2O_5$
   b. $2\ P_4 + 5\ O_2 \rightarrow 1\ P_2O_5$
   c. $2\ P_4 + 5\ O_2 \rightarrow 7\ P_2O_5$
   d. $1\ P_4 + 5\ O_2 \rightarrow 2\ P_2O_5$

34. A pulley lifts a 5 kg object 10 m into the air in 5 seconds. How much power is used?
   a. 50 J
   b. 50 N
   c. 98.1 J
   d. 98.1 W

35. What is the formula for carbon tetraiodide?
   a. C_4I
   b. CI_4
   c. C_2I_4
   d. CI

36. What kind of bond is formed between the two atoms shown in the periodic table below?

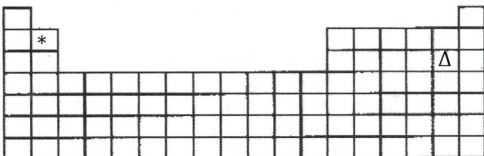

a. a covalent bond
b. an ionic bond
c. a metallic bond
d. a non-metallic bond

37. What mathematical expression can be used to calculate the volume in liters of two moles of an ideal gas at STP? R = 8.314 L·kPa / K·mol

a. $V = \frac{(2)(8.314)(273)}{100}$

b. $V = (100)(2)(8.314)(273)$

c. $V = \frac{(2)(8.314)(0)}{100}$

d. $V = \frac{(2)(8.314)(0)}{1}$

38. What category of chemical reaction is the reaction below?
$$P_4 + 5O_2 \rightarrow P_4O_{10}$$
a. synthesis
b. decomposition
c. single replacement
d. double replacement

39. Which of the following *unbalanced* chemical equations is an oxidation-reduction reaction?
a. $Al + O_2 \rightarrow Al_2O_3$
b. $Hg_2(NO_3)_2 + K_2SO_4 \rightarrow Hg_2SO_4 + KNO_3$
c. $K + Cl_2 \rightarrow KCl$
d. $HgO \rightarrow Hg + O_2$

40. Which combination of household chemicals produces a toxic gas?
a. baking soda and vinegar
b. bleach and ammonia
c. water and sugar
d. vinegar and antacid tablets

41. A solution is made by dissolving 87.75 grams of NaCl into 500 mL of water. What is the final concentration of the NaCl?
a. 0.176 molar
b. 0.33 molar
c. 3 molar
d. 3.16 molar

42. A teaspoon of sugar is dissolved in a glass of water. The solution in the glass is ____:
a. an atom
b. a compound
c. an element
d. a mixture

43. A perfectly circular track has a circumference of 400 meters. A runner goes around the track in 100 seconds instead of her usual time of 80 seconds because a leg cramp causes her to stop running for 20 seconds. What is her average speed?
    a. 0 m/s
    b. 5 m/s
    c. 4 m/s
    d. 20 m/s

44. Which of the following demonstrations best illustrates Newton's first law?
    a. Giving a billiard ball at rest on a smooth level table a small push and letting it roll on the table.
    b. Dragging a box on a table at a constant speed by exerting a force just enough to overcome the force of friction.
    c. Trying without success to move a heavy bureau or filing cabinet on the floor.
    d. Running a current through two parallel wires.

45. The force of gravity on Earth's moon is 1/6 the force of gravity on the Earth. The force due to gravity on Earth is 9.81 m/s². What is the weight of a 5 kg mass on the moon?
    a. 0.833 N
    b. 8.175 N
    c. 30.00 N
    d. 49.05 N

46. Review the graph below. Which statement correctly describes what is happening to the object?

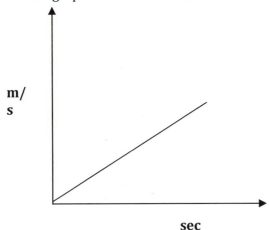

    a. The object has constant velocity.
    b. The object has constant acceleration.
    c. The object is at rest. It is not moving.
    d. The object has increasing acceleration.

47. An object begins its motion at (0,0). It moves +5 units on the x axis and then -3 units on the y axis. Which vector represents the displacement of the object?

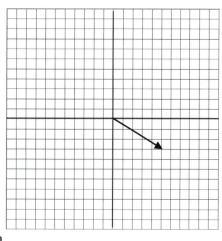

a.

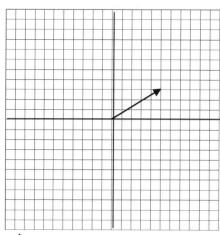

b.

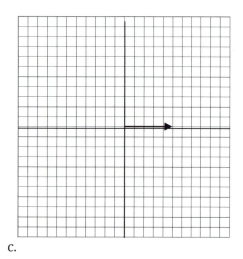

c.

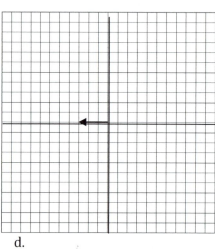

d.

48. What is the definition of work?
    a. the amount of energy used to accomplish a job
    b. the force used to move a mass over a distance
    c. the amount of power per unit of time
    d. energy stored in an object due to its position

49. A pulley lifts a 10 kg object 10 m into the air in 5 minutes. Using this information you can calculate:
    a. mechanical advantage
    b. efficiency
    c. frictional resistance
    d. power

50. Semiconductors belong to what group of elements?
    a. alkaline earth metals
    b. halogens
    c. metalloids
    d. noble gases

51. Which mathematical expression can be used to calculate the *total* resistance in a series circuit?
    a. $R_{eq} = R_1 + R_2 + \cdots + R_n$

    b. $\dfrac{1}{R_{eq}} = \dfrac{1}{R_1} + \dfrac{1}{R_2} + \cdots + \dfrac{1}{R_n}$

    c. $R = \dfrac{\rho l}{A}$

    d. $C = Q / V$

52. Which of the following creates a magnetic field?
    a. the spinning and rotating of electrons in atoms
    b. the separation of charged particles in atoms
    c. the vibrational and translational motion of atoms
    d. loosely held valence electrons surrounding an atom

53. Which of the following materials has randomly aligned dipoles?
    a. a non-magnetic substance
    b. an electromagnet
    c. a permanent magnet
    d. a horseshoe magnet

54. What property of light explains why a pencil in a glass of water appears to be bent?
    a. reflection
    b. refraction
    c. angle of incidence = angle of reflection
    d. constructive interference

55. What unit describes the frequency of a wave?
    a. hertz (Hz)
    b. decibels (dB)
    c. meters (m)
    d. meters per second (m/s)

56. What wave characteristic determines if electromagnetic radiation is in the form of a radio wave or an X-ray?
    a. frequency
    b. amplitude
    c. wavelength
    d. speed of light

57. Which of the following is true about a diffraction grating?
   a. The more slits per inch, the greater the amount of destructive interference.
   b. Blue light diffracts more than red light in a diffraction grating.
   c. A diffraction grating produces maxima and minima only for monochromatic light.
   d. Light passing through a diffraction grating produces a bulls-eye pattern.

58. What wave characteristic is related to the pitch of a sound?
   a. frequency
   b. amplitude
   c. wavelength
   d. speed of sound

59. What wave characteristic is related to the loudness of a sound?
   a. frequency
   b. amplitude
   c. wavelength
   d. speed of sound

60. What unit describes the loudness of a sound?
   a. hertz (Hz)
   b. decibels (dB)
   c. meters (m)
   d. meters per second (m/s)

61. Which of the following organelles is/are formed when the plasma membrane surrounds a particle outside of the cell?
   a. Rough endoplasmic reticulum
   b. Lysosomes
   c. Secretory vesicles
   d. Endocytic vesicles

62. Which of the following plant organelles contain(s) pigment that give leaves their color?
   a. Centrioles
   b. Cell walls
   c. Chloroplasts
   d. Central vacuole

63. All but which of the following processes are ways of moving solutes across a plasma membrane?
   a. Osmosis
   b. Passive transport
   c. Active transport
   d. Facilitated diffusion

64. Prokaryotic and eukaryotic cells are similar in having which of the following?
   a. Membrane-bound organelles
   b. Protein-studded DNA
   c. Presence of a nucleus
   d. Integral membrane proteins in the plasma membrane

65. How many chromosomes does a human cell have after meiosis I?
    a. 92
    b. 46
    c. 23
    d. 22

66. DNA replication occurs during which of the following phases?
    a. Prophase I
    b. Prophase II
    c. Interphase I
    d. Interphase II

67. Enzymes catalyze biochemical reactions by
    a. Lowering the potential energy of the products
    b. Separating inhibitors from products
    c. Forming a complex with the products
    d. Lowering the activation energy of the reaction

68. Which of the following is not a characteristic of enzymes?
    a. They change shape when they bind their substrates
    b. They can catalyze reactions in both forward and reverse directions
    c. Their activity is sensitive to changes in temperature
    d. They are always active on more than one kind of substrate

69. In photosynthesis, high-energy electrons move through electron transport chains to produce ATP and NADPH. Which of the following provides the energy to create high energy electrons?
    a. NADH
    b. NADP+
    c. Water
    d. Light

70. In plants and animals, genetic variation is introduced during
    a. Crossing over in mitosis
    b. Chromosome segregation in mitosis
    c. Cytokinesis of meiosis
    d. Anaphase I of meiosis

71. A length of DNA coding for a particular protein is called a(n)
    a. Allele
    b. Genome
    c. Gene
    d. Transcript

72. Which of the following chemical moieties forms the backbone of DNA?
    a. Nitrogenous bases
    b. Glycerol
    c. Amino groups
    d. Pentose and phosphate

73. Required for the activity of DNA polymerase
    a. Okazaki fragments
    b. RNA primer
    c. Single-strand binding protein
    d. Leading strand

74. Which of the following of Lamarck's evolutionary ideas turned out to be true?
    a. Natural selection
    b. Organisms naturally transform into increasingly complex organisms
    c. Inheritance of acquired characters
    d. Body parts develop with increased usage and weaken with disuse

75. The weight of adult wolves is within a fairly narrow range, even if they are well-fed in zoos. This is an example of
    a. Stabilizing selection
    b. Directional selection
    c. Disruptive selection
    d. Sexual selection

76. Which of the following conditions would promote evolutionary change?
    a. Random mating
    b. A large population
    c. An isolated population
    d. Gene flow

77. On a standard biomass pyramid, level 3 corresponds to which trophic level?
    a. Producers
    b. Decomposers
    c. Primary consumers
    d. Primary carnivores

78. Which of the following parts of an angiosperm give rise to the fruit?
    a. Pedicel
    b. Filament
    c. Sepal
    d. Ovary

79. Which of the following structures is NOT present in gymnosperms?
    a. Leaves
    b. Pollen
    c. Flowers
    d. Stomata

80. When an animal takes in more energy that it uses over an extended time, the extra chemical energy is stored as:
    a. Fat
    b. Starch
    c. Protein
    d. Enzymes

81. Animals exchange gases with the environment in all of the following ways EXCEPT
   a. Direct exchange through the skin
   b. Exchange through gills
   c. Stomata
   d. Tracheae

82. Which of the following is the major way in which carbon is released into the environment?
   a. Transpiration
   b. Respiration
   c. Fixation
   d. Sedimentation

83. What is the largest reservoir of nitrogen on the planet?
   a. The ocean
   b. Plants
   c. Soil
   d. The atmosphere

84. A population of 1000 individuals has 110 births and 10 deaths in a year. Its growth rate (r) is equal to
   a. 0.01 per year
   b. 0.1 per year
   c. 0.09 per year
   d. 0.11 per year

85. Which of the following statements correctly describes a similarity or difference between rocks and minerals?
   a. Minerals may contain traces of organic compounds, while rocks do not.
   b. Rocks are classified by their formation and the minerals they contain, while minerals are classified by their chemical composition and physical properties.
   c. Both rocks and minerals can be polymorphs.
   d. Both rocks and minerals may contain mineraloids.

86. Which of the following is the best description of mineraloids?
   a. Mineraloids are organic compounds found in rocks.
   b. Mineraloids are inorganic solids containing two or more minerals with different crystalline structures.
   c. Mineraloids are inorganic solids containing one or more minerals with the same crystalline structure.
   d. Mineraloids are minerals that lack a crystalline structure.

87. Which of the following is NOT one of the five major physical properties of minerals?
   a. Chemical composition
   b. Hardness
   c. Luster
   d. Streak

88. Which of these minerals would have the lowest score on the Mohs scale?
   a. Gypsum
   b. Fluorite
   c. Talc
   d. Diamond

89. A mineral's true color is observed by:
   a. Conducting a streak test on white paper.
   b. Conducting a streak test on unglazed porcelain tile.
   c. Inspecting the mineral's outer surface.
   d. Shining a light on the mineral to inspect its luster.

90. The lithification process results in the formation of which of the following types of rocks?
   a. Sedimentary
   b. Intrusive igneous
   c. Extrusive igneous
   d. Metamorphic

91. Which of the following factors directly contributes to soil erosion?
   a. Air pollution from cars and factories
   b. Use of pesticides
   c. Deforestation and overgrazing
   d. Water pollution caused by excess sedimentation

92. Physical weathering of rocks can be caused by all of the following EXCEPT:
   a. The freezing and thawing of water on the surface of rocks.
   b. Changes in temperature.
   c. Oxidation.
   d. Changes in pressure due to the removal of overlying rocks.

93. Which of the following types of igneous rock solidifies deepest beneath the Earth's surface?
   a. Hypabyssal
   b. Plutonic
   c. Volcanic
   d. Detrital

94. Which of the following is required for the process of diagenesis (also called lithification)?
   a. Magma
   b. Water
   c. Wind
   d. Sulfur

95. Water that evaporates from oceans can precipitate over land due to the process of:
   a. Transpiration.
   b. Advection.
   c. Sublimation.
   d. Interception.

96. Water is likely to have the shortest residence time in which of the following types of reservoirs?
    a. A glacier
    b. A lake
    c. A river
    d. The atmosphere

97. In 1912, Alfred Wegener proposed that:
    a. The Earth's magnetic poles have reversed several times throughout history.
    b. Tectonic plates move because of convection currents in the mantle.
    c. Mountains are formed by tectonic plates pushing against one another.
    d. The continents once formed a single land mass, but have since drifted apart.

98. Which of the following is a true statement about the Earth's oceans?
    a. Oceans comprise about 50 percent of the Earth's surface.
    b. The deepest point in the ocean is about 6,000 meters below sea level.
    c. The ocean is divided geographically into four areas: the Atlantic, Pacific, Mediterranean, and Indian.
    d. The ocean's salinity is usually between 34 and 35 parts per thousand, or 200 parts per million.

99. A guyot is defined as:
    a. Any undersea mountain more than 1,000 meters high.
    b. A seamount with a flattened top.
    c. An undersea mountain chain.
    d. A trough in the ocean floor.

100. Approximately 96.5 percent of seawater is comprised of:
    a. Hydrogen and sodium.
    b. Hydrogen and oxygen.
    c. Oxygen and sodium.
    d. Chlorine and sodium.

101. Which of the following statements correctly describes a difference between surface and subsurface ocean currents?
    a. Subsurface currents are caused only by temperature variations, while surface currents are caused by changes in air pressure.
    b. Subsurface currents are caused by temperature and density variations, while surface currents are caused by changes in air pressure.
    c. Subsurface currents are caused by temperature and density variations, while surface currents are caused by wind.
    d. Surface currents are caused by changes in air temperature, while subsurface currents are caused by changes in water temperature.

102. Which of the following statements correctly describes a difference between the lithosphere and the asthenosphere?

a. The asthenosphere is comprised of atmospheric gas, while the lithosphere is composed of liquids and solids.

b. The asthenosphere is hotter and more fluid than the lithosphere.

c. The lithosphere is hotter and has a different chemical composition than the asthenosphere.

d. Heat is transferred through conduction in the asthenosphere, while it is transferred through convection in the lithosphere.

103. The majority of weather phenomena occur in which part of the Earth's atmosphere?

a. Troposphere

b. Stratosphere

c. Hydrosphere

d. Ionosphere

104. According to the Köppen Climate Classification System, regions with continental climates are most commonly found:

a. In the interior regions of large landmasses.

b. Near the equator.

c. Near the Earth's poles.

d. In places with high temperatures year-round.

105. Which of the following planets in our solar system is NOT a gas giant?

a. Saturn

b. Neptune

c. Venus

d. Jupiter

106. How is light created in the core of the sun?

a. convection

b. fission reactions

c. fusion reactions

d. chemical reactions

107. Which of the following is considered observational evidence in support of the Big Bang Theory?

a. Expansion in the redshifts of galaxies

b. Measurements of cosmic microwave background radiation

c. Measurements of the distribution of quasars and galaxies

d. All of the above

108. Redshift is observed when:

a. A light-emitting object moves away from an observer.

b. A star begins to decrease the amount of light it emits.

c. A light-emitting object moves toward an observer.

d. A magnetic field bends observed light.

109. When students are taught science, the information needs to be ____.
    a. correct, contextualized, and explained.
    b. diverse, multicultural, and functional.
    c. demonstrated, teacher-prepared, and manipulative.
    d. theoretical, practical, and researched.

110. Which of the following demographic changes would lead to a population with an older age composition?
    a. Increased birth rate
    b. Environmental pollution
    c. Increased availability of food
    d. Medical advancements that increase life expectancy

111. Which of the following factors has the greatest impact on birth rate in humans?
    a. Age at reproductive maturity
    b. Reproductive lifetime
    c. Survivorship of offspring to reproductive maturity
    d. Socioeconomic factors

112. Clear-cutting of rain forests leads to all of the following consequences EXCEPT
    a. Climate change
    b. Erosion
    c. Reduction in species diversity
    d. Air pollution

113. Burning fossil fuels releases sulfur dioxide and nitrogen dioxide. These pollutants lead to which environmental problem?
    a. Denitrification
    b. Acid rain
    c. Global climate change
    d. Ozone depletion

114. The main manmade cause of "dead zones" in portions of oceans and lakes that normally host abundant aquatic life is:
    a. Evaporation.
    b. Invasive species.
    c. Use of chemical fertilizers.
    d. Global warming.

115. Which type of aberration does not occur with concave spherical mirrors?
    a. Astigmatism
    b. Chromatic aberration
    c. Spherical aberration
    d. Distortion

116. A calorimeter is used to measure changes in:
    a. Heat.
    b. Mass.
    c. Weight.
    d. Volume.

117. Commercial nuclear reactors generate electricity through the process of:
    a. Nuclear fission.
    b. Nuclear fusion.
    c. Nuclear depletion.
    d. Radioactive decay.

118. The Environmental Protection Agency issues reports on the condition of:
    a. wetlands
    b. watersheds
    c. floodplains
    d. All of the above

119. The treatment of hazardous waste includes:
    a. neutralizing the substance
    b. recovering energy
    c. preparing waste for disposal
    d. All of the above

120. About 25 years ago, a study appeared to demonstrate a strong relationship between drinking coffee and developing a variety of different cancers. What was the problem with this study?
    a. It failed to take into account the amount of coffee consumed daily by the subjects of the study.
    b. It failed to take into account whether the coffee consumed by the subjects of the study was caffeinated or not.
    c. It failed to take into account the temperature of the coffee consumed by the subjects of the study.
    d. It failed to take into account whether the subjects of the study were also smokers or consumed alcoholic beverages.

Answers and Explanations

1. A: Descriptive studies are usually the first form of study in a new area of scientific inquiry. Others are also forms of scientific study, but are completed after initial descriptive studies.

2. A: The purpose of conducting an experiment is to test a hypothesis. Answer choices b, c, and d are steps in conducting an experiment designed to test a hypothesis. .

3. A: The prefix milli- means 1/1000 and liter is the basic metric unit of volume. Answer choice b is incorrect because the prefix centi- means 1/100 and the gram is the basic unit of mass. Answer choice c is incorrect because the prefix kilo means 1000 and the gallon is not a metric unit of volume. Answer choice d is incorrect because the prefix deci- means 1/10 and the quart is not a metric unit of volume.

4. A: The conversion is done as follows: (25.4 cm) x (1in/2.54 cm) = 10 inches.
Answer choice b is arrived at by using the following incorrect formula: (25.4 cm) x (1 foot / 12 cm).
Answer choice c is arrived at by using the following incorrect formula: (25.4 cm) x (1 meter/10 cm).
Converting from cm to m requires the use of the following formula: (cm) x (1 m / 100 cm).
Answer choice d is arrived at by using the following incorrect formula: (25.4 cm) x (100 mm / 1 cm). Converting from cm to mm requires the use of the following formula: (cm) x (10 mm / 1 cm).

5. A: Repeating a measurement several times can increase the accuracy of the measurement. Calibrating the equipment (b) will increase the precision of the measurement. None of the other choices are useful strategies to increase the accuracy of a measurement.

6. A: A correlational study of a population is an example of a descriptive study. Answer choices b and c are examples of the controlled experimentation type of scientific investigation. Answer choice d is an example of the comparative data analysis type of scientific investigation.

7. A: The force of gravity points straight down. The normal force is perpendicular to the surface of the block. The force of friction points down the slope. The only one of these diagrams with all three vectors pointing in those directions is answer A.

8. C: Acid should always be added to water, creating a mixture with an increasing concentration. Since the mixture of a strong acid with water generates heat, the addition of water directly to acid could cause the solution, which would initially have a very high concentration of acid, to boil and possibly splash upward, creating a hazardous condition.

9. D: A CAD program can be used in a laboratory setting to generate graphical models. Collecting digital data (a) requires the use of computer probes. Lab reports (b) are written up using a word processing program. Creating lab instructions (c) and reducing statistical error are not applications of a CAD program.

10. A: Using containers for broken glassware is recommended but not required by law. The other safety requirements listed are required by state law.

11. A: This sign shows the material contained on a Material Safety Data Sheet (MSDS). The graphic in b is a generic *do not mix chemicals* warning. The graphic in c is a sign denoting the *location of the emergency exit*. The graphic in d is a sign denoting the *location of the fire extinguisher*.

12. C: Ibn Hayyan, Lavoisier, Mendeleev, and Curie are associated with the study of chemistry. The scientists listed in choice a are associated with the study of physics. The scientists listed in choice b are associated with the study of biology. The scientists listed in choice d are associated with the study of geology.

13. D: Protons and electrons are constituents of atoms. The precise numbers of protons, electrons, and neutrons in an atom define the various elements which can combine to form compounds and molecules.

14. B: Magnesium and strontium are both in group IIA of the periodic table. They are alkaline earth metals, which have similar chemical properties.

15. A: The center of an atom is known as the nucleus. It is composed of protons and neutrons.

16. A: Isotopes are two atoms of the same element that have different mass. They have the same number of protons but a different number of neutrons. Choice c accurately describes ions. The other choices are incorrect.

17. A: The correct electron configuration for an atom of nitrogen is $1s^2 2s^2 2p^3$.

18. A: The arrow is pointing to the atomic number, which also indicates the number of protons the element contains.

19. A: Alpha particles are essentially helium nuclei with a mass of 4 amu. Beta rays (b) are electrons released when a neutron decomposes to form a proton and an electron. The mass of an electron (beta) is approximately $1/2000^{th}$ amu. Gamma rays (c) are high energy, short wavelength, high frequency electromagnetic waves. Gamma rays have no mass. X-rays (d) are also electromagnetic waves and have no mass.

20. A: Lead 210 has a mass of 210 amu and an atomic number of 82. The starting material in the equation is $^{210}_{82}Pb$; beta emission is represented by e^- on the right side of the arrow. The mass of the final product does not change. However, the proton number increases by one. Answer b is incorrect because an atom with 83 protons is not Pb, but Bi. Answers c and d are incorrect because they contain an alpha particle instead of a beta ray.

21. A: After 38.2 days, 10 half-lives have occurred. This means that $1/2^{10}$ remains of the original sample. This is equivalent to 1/1024 of a gram.

22. C: One calorie is the amount of heat energy required to increase the temperature of 1 gram of water by 1 degree C. The test taker needs to know that the specific heat of water is 1 cal/g °C. The correct calculation to solve this problem is:

(amount of water) x (specific heat of water) x (temperature change of water)

OR

(100 g) x (1 cal / g °C) x (55°C – 50°C) = 500 calories

23. A: The mathematical formula for linear expansion is: $\Delta L = \alpha L_0 \Delta T$. Choice a correctly inserts the values provided in the table into this equation. Choice b is incorrect because it uses the coefficient of *volume* expansion. Choice c is incorrect because it uses density and then cubes the length of the

rod in an attempt to rectify mismatched units. Choice d is incorrect because it cubes the length of the rod, converts from inches to centimeters, and converts from Kelvin to °C.

24. A: The magnitude of the temperature on the Fahrenheit scale is calculated using the mathematical expression °F = (9/5)°C + 32. At the boiling point of water, 100 °C, the temperature in Fahrenheit is calculated to be 212 °F. Kelvin (absolute temperature) is calculated using the mathematical expression K = °C + 273. At 100 °C, the temperature in Kelvin is 373 K. Thus, the order from least to greatest is 100 °C, 212 °F, 373 K

25. A: Phase changes are physical changes, not chemical changes (b). Sublimation (c) occurs when a solid turns directly to a gas without passing through the liquid state. Condensation (d) occurs when a gas turns to liquid.

26. D: The noble gases (inert gases) have full electron shells, which makes them chemically stable atoms.

27. A: The addition of energy causes a phase change. Phase changes are physical changes, not chemical changes. While sublimation is an example of a phase change, it occurs when a solid turns directly to a gas without passing through the liquid state. Condensation, another phase change, occurs when a gas turns to liquid. Single replacement reactions are one category of chemical change.

28. C: This is the group containing halogens, which are highly reactive and need only one electron to fill their outer shells. Group a are the alkali metals, which are highly reactive but have only 1 electron in their outer shells. Group b are the alkaline earth metals, which have 2 electrons in their outer shells. Group d are the noble gases, which are inert and have full outer electron shells.

29. B: Temperature is a measure of the kinetic energy of particles. As temperature increases the average kinetic energy also increases. As the gas particles move more rapidly they occupy a larger volume. The increase in speed of the individual particles combined with the greater distance over which any intermolecular forces must act results in a decrease in the intermolecular forces.

30. D: The combined gas law is mathematically expressed as $\frac{P_1 V_1}{T_1} = \frac{P_2 V_2}{T_2}$ OR $V_2 = \frac{P_1 V_1 T_2}{T_1 P_2}$.

Those who chose answer choice a incorrectly solved the mathematical expression as $V_2 = \frac{P_1 V_1 P_2}{T_1 T_2}$.

Those who chose answer choice b incorrectly solved the mathematical expression as $V_2 = \frac{P_2 T_1}{P_1 V_1 T_2}$ and failed to convert the temperature from °C to K.

Those who chose answer choice c incorrectly solved the mathematical expression as $V_2 = \frac{V_1 T_1}{P_1 P_2 T_2}$.

Only those who chose answer d used the correct values and rearranged the expression in the correct way.

31. D: The sodium ion has a 1+ charge (Na^+). The phosphate ion has a 3- charge $(PO_4)^{3-}$. Using the criss-cross rule, it can be determined that three sodiums will balance the charge on one phosphate. Na_3PO_4 is correct.
The test taker who does not recognize phosphate as PO_4 may be drawn to choice a or b.
The test-taker who does not recognize the symbol for sodium as Na may be drawn to choice b.
The test-taker who does not remember the criss-cross rule may be drawn to choice c.

32. C: An aluminum ion has a 3+ charge (Al^{3+}). A sulfate ion has a 2- charge (SO_4)$^{2-}$. Using the criss-cross rule, three aluminums will balance the charge on two sulfates. Therefore, $Al_2(SO_4)_3$ is the correct answer.

33. D: When balancing a chemical reaction, the goal is to get an equal number of each type of atom on both sides of the reaction. The atoms that are there to begin with (reactants) must also be present at the end of the reaction (products). Answer choice d has 4 phosphorus atoms and 10 oxygen atoms on both sides.

34. D: The unit of power is watts (W). The mathematical formula used to calculate power is power = work/time OR power = [(mass x gravity) x (distance)]/time. Using the values in the question, this equation gives
[(5 kg x 9.81 m/s^2) x (10 m)]/5 s = 98.1 kg-m^2/s^3 OR 98.1 J/s OR 98.1 W.

35. B: The valence of iodine is 1⁻, while that of carbon is 4⁺. To follow the octet rule, the covalent compound carbon tetratiodide must have four atoms of iodine and a single atom of carbon.

36. B: Ionic bonds form between metals and nonmetals. * is an alkaline earth metal. Δ is a halogen, a non-metal.

37. A: Finding the correct answer to this item requires the test taker to be aware of and use the following pieces of information:
- The mathematical expression known as the Ideal Gas Law is PV = nRT, where P is the pressure of the gas, V is the volume of the gas, n is the number of moles of the gas, R is the gas constant, and T is the temperature of the gas measured in Kelvin.
- The algebraic rearrangement of the expression yields the formula V = nRT/P.
- STP = 273K and 100 kPa

Answer choice b incorrectly solves for V in the Ideal Gas Law. Answer choice c fails to convert from °C to K. Answer choice d interprets STP as 1 atm and fails to convert the pressure to kPa.

38. A: In a synthesis reaction, simpler compounds are combined to form a more complex compound.

39. A: $Al + O_2 \rightarrow Al_2O_3$ is an example of an oxidation reaction.
Answer choice b is a double replacement reaction.
Answer choice c is a synthesis reaction.
Answer choice d is a decomposition reaction.

40. B: When combined, bleach and ammonia release chlorine gas. Baking soda and vinegar (a) release carbon dioxide gas bubbles. Sugar simply dissolves in water (c). Vinegar (acetic acid) is neutralized by antacid tablets in a double replacement reaction that produces water (d).

41. C: Concentration is defined as the number of moles per liter of volume. Therefore, 87.75 g of NaCl = 1.5 moles of NaCl; 1.5 moles of NaCl / 0.5 L of H_2O = 3 molar.
The test-taker who chooses a completed the calculation as follows: (87.85 g NaCl/500 mL H_2O).
The test-taker who chooses b inverted the calculation as follows: (0.5 L H_2O / 1.5 moles NaCl).
The test-taker who chooses d made several errors: converting the volume of water to 27.7 moles using the incorrect calculation (500 mL/18 g/mol) and subsequently dividing the moles of water into 87.85 gram of NaCl.

42. D: Sugar water is a mixture. The solution can be separated into its component parts. Evaporation will remove the water and leave the sugar in the glass.

43 C: The average speed is the total distance (400 m) divided by the total time spent travelling (100 s). Answer A would be correct if the question asked for the instantaneous velocity while the runner was stopped. Answer B is the runner's average speed when running at her usual time, finishing the race in 80 seconds. Answer D is the average speed if the runner had completed the race in 20 seconds, not 100.

44. A: Newton's first law (inertia) says an object in motion stays in motion, and an object at rest stays at rest, unless external forces act on them. I is an excellent demonstration because it shows the ball at rest and in motion. At rest, the ball stays at rest until a force acts on it. When the ball is moving, there is no force acting on the ball in the direction of motion. Thus, the natural state of the ball is to be at rest or moving with a constant speed. Answer C is not a good demonstration because the force of friction is what makes it hard to move the heavy object. Answer B is a good demonstration of equilibrium and friction. Answer D, running a current through wires, has nothing to do with Newton's first law.

45. B: Weight is the force of gravity acting on a mass. The combination of Newton's 1st and 2nd Laws of Motion yields the mathematical formula $F = ma$. Applied to weight, this relationship can also be expressed as $F = mg$. To arrive at the correct answer, first multiply Earth's gravity by 1/6 to calculate the gravity on the moon ($g = 9.81$ m/s^2 x 1/6 = 1.635 m/s^2). The second step is to multiply this value by the mass of the object ($F = 5$ kg x 1.635m/s^2; F=8.175N).

The test taker who chooses a multiplied the mass by 1/6 and ignored the gravity component altogether. The test taker who chooses c divided the mass by 1/6 and ignored the gravity component altogether. The test taker who chooses d calculated the mass of the object on Earth and ignored the variable of the moon.

46. B: The line on the velocity time graph represents acceleration. The slope indicates a constant rate of acceleration. The test taker who does not recognize the units on the y-axis (m/s) as velocity may incorrectly choose option a. The test taker who equates an upward slope with an increasing value may be drawn to option d.

47. A: Vector addition involves the "head to tail" rule. The starting point is (0, 0). Moving five units to the right and three units down will bring the test taker to the end point. When these two points are connected the resulting vector is the one pictured in answer choice a.

48. B: Work is defined as the force used to move a mass over a distance. Choice a may be a secular (non-scientific) definition of work. Choice c is the definition of power. Choice d is the definition of potential energy.

49. D: Power = work / time. The mass of the object (10 kg) and the distance (10 m) can be used to calculate work. The value for time is also provided.

50. C: Metalloids have some properties of metals and some properties of nonmetals. A good semiconductor has the conductive properties of metals and a stability at high temperatures that is characteristic of nonmetals.

51. A: This expression can be used to calculate the total resistance in a series circuit. Choice b is the mathematical expression to calculate total resistance in a parallel series. Choice c is the mathematical expression to calculate resistance in a uniformly shaped material. Choice d is the mathematical expression to calculate capacitance (stored electric charge).

52. A: A magnetic field is created by a spin magnetic dipole moment and the orbital magnetic dipole moment of the electrons in atoms. Therefore, it is the spinning and rotating of electrons in atoms that creates a magnetic field. Choice b describes the nucleus and electron clouds within an atom. Choice c creates thermal energy. Choice d creates a good electrical conductor.

53. A: Magnetic poles occur in pairs known as magnetic dipoles. Individual atoms can be considered magnetic dipoles due to the spinning and rotation of the electrons in the atoms. When the dipoles are aligned, the material is magnetic. Choices b, c, and d are all magnetic materials. Therefore, the magnetic dipoles in these materials are NOT randomly aligned. Only choice a has randomly aligned dipoles.

54. B: Light travels in straight lines. As light moves from one substance to another, the light rays bend according to the refractive index of each substance. As the light travels through the air, it hits the non-submerged portion of the pencil. The light is reflected from the pencil and this is what we see. However, as the light travels *into* the water, the light waves are bent (refracted), and that light is subsequently reflected and travels to our eyes. What we perceive is a pencil that is no longer whole and straight, but broken and bent. It is refraction (choice b) that causes this perception. Although the other distractors are also properties of waves, they are not the reasons why the observer perceives the pencil as bent.

55. A: Hertz (Hz) is a unit of measure of wave frequency.
The loudness of a sound is related to the amplitude of the wave and is measured in decibels (dB).
Wavelength is measured in meters (m).
Wave velocity is measured in meters per second (m/s).

56. C: Wavelength determines the nature of the electromagnetic wave (i.e. radio waves, microwaves, infrared radiation, visible light, ultraviolet radiation, X-rays, gamma rays, etc.).
Sound pitch depends on the frequency (a) of the sound wave.
The loudness of a sound depends on the amplitude (b) of the sound wave.
The speed of light (d) is a constant.

57. A: Diffraction gratings produce so much destructive interference that large distances separate the bright lines due to interference. This means diffraction gratings can be used to separate light consisting of different wave lengths. Answer B is wrong because blue light, which has a shorter wavelength than red light, refracts and diffracts less than red light. The greater the wavelength of light, the more it changes direction when it hits an edge.

58. A: Sound pitch depends on the frequency of the sound wave.
The loudness of a sound depends on the amplitude of the sound wave (b).
Wavelength (c) determines the nature of the electromagnetic wave (i.e. radio waves, microwaves, infrared radiation, visible light, ultraviolet radiation, X-rays, gamma rays, etc.).
The speed of sound (d) is a constant for any specific medium. For example, the speed of sound in air is 340 m/s.

59. B: The loudness of a sound depends on the amplitude of the sound wave.

Sound pitch depends on the frequency (a) of the sound wave.

Wavelength (c) determines the nature of the electromagnetic wave (i.e. radio waves, microwaves, infrared radiation, visible light, ultraviolet radiation, X-rays, gamma rays, etc.).

The speed of sound (d) is a constant for any specific medium. For example, the speed of sound in air is 340 m/s.

60. B: The loudness of a sound is related to the amplitude of the wave and is measured in decibels (dB).

Wave frequency is measured in Hertz (Hz).

Wavelength is measured in meters (m).

Wave velocity is measured in meters per second (m/s).

61. D: Endocytosis is a process by which cells absorb larger molecules or even tiny organisms, such as bacteria, than would be able to pass through the plasma membrane. Endocytic vesicles containing molecules from the extracellular environment often undergo further processing once they enter the cell.

62. C: Chloroplasts contain the light-absorbing compound chlorophyll, which is essential in photosynthesis. This gives leaves their green color. Chloroplasts also contain yellow and red carotenoid pigments, which give leaves red and yellow colors in the fall as chloroplasts lose their chlorophyll.

63. A: Osmosis is the movement of water molecules (not solutes) across a semi-permeable membrane. Water moves from a region of higher concentration to a region of lower concentration. Osmosis occurs when the concentrations of a solute differ on either side of a semi-permeable membrane. For example, a cell (containing a higher concentration of water) in a salty solution (containing a lower concentration of water) will lose water as water leaves the cell. This continues until the solution outside the cell has the same salt concentration as the cytoplasm.

64. D: Both prokaryotes and eukaryotes interact with the extracellular environment and use membrane-bound or membrane-associated proteins to achieve this. They both use diffusion and active transport to move materials in and out of their cells. Prokaryotes have very few proteins associated with their DNA, whereas eukaryotes' DNA is richly studded with proteins. Both types of living things can have flagella, although with different structural characteristics in the two groups. The most important differences between prokaryotes and eukaryotes are the lack of a nucleus and membrane-bound organelles in prokaryotes.

65. B: The diploid chromosome number for humans is 46. After DNA duplication but before the first cell division of meiosis, there are 92 chromosomes (46 pairs). After meiosis I is completed, the chromosome number is halved and equals 46. Each daughter cell is haploid, but the chromosomes are still paired (sister chromatids). During meiosis II, the two sister chromatids of each chromosome separate, resulting in 23 haploid chromosomes per germ cell.

66. C: Although there are two cell divisions in meiosis, DNA replication occurs only once. It occurs in interphase I, before M phase begins.

67. D: Enzymes act as catalysts for biochemical reactions. A catalyst is not consumed in a reaction, but, rather, lowers the activation energy for that reaction. The potential energy of the substrate and the product remain the same, but the activation energy—the energy needed to make the reaction progress—can be lowered with the help of an enzyme.

- 31 -

68. D: Enzymes are substrate-specific. Most enzymes catalyze only one biochemical reaction. Their active sites are specific for a certain type of substrate and do not bind to other substrates and catalyze other reactions.

69. D: Electrons trapped by the chlorophyll P680 molecule in photosystem II are energized by light. They are then transferred to electron acceptors in an electron transport chain.

70. D: In anaphase I, homologous chromosome pairs segregate randomly into daughter cells. This means that each daughter cell contains a unique combination of chromosomes that is different from the mother cell and different from its cognate daughter cell.

71. C: Genes code for proteins, and genes are discrete lengths of DNA on chromosomes. An allele is a variant of a gene (different DNA sequence.. In diploid organisms, there may be two versions of each gene.

72. D: DNA is composed of nucleotides joined together in long chains. Nucleotides are composed of a pentose sugar, a phosphate group, and a nitrogenous base. The bases form the "rungs" of the ladder at the core of the DNA helix and the pentose-phosphates are on its outside, or backbone.

73. B: DNA replication begins with a short segment of RNA (not DNA.. DNA polymerase cannot begin adding nucleotides without an existing piece of DNA (a primer).

74. D: Natural selection was Darwin's idea, not Lamarck's. Mendel discovered that genes are the basic units of inheritance. Lamarck's observation about use and disuse is true, although he did not connect it with the underlying mechanism of natural selection.

75. A: Stabilizing selection is a form of selection in which a particular trait, such as weight, becomes stable within a population. It results in reduced genetic variability, and the disappearance of alleles for extreme traits. Over time, the most common phenotypes survive.

76. D: Options a, b, and c all describe conditions that would lead to genetic equilibrium, where no evolution would occur. Gene flow, which is the introduction or removal of alleles from a population, would allow natural selection to work and could promote evolutionary change.

77. D: At the lowest trophic level are the producers, followed by primary consumers. Primary carnivores follow consumers, followed by secondary carnivores.

78. D: The ovary houses the ovules in a flower. Pollen grains fertilize ovules to create seeds, and the ovary matures into a fruit.

79. C: Gymnosperms reproduce by producing pollen and ovules, but they do not have flowers. Instead, their reproductive structures are cones or cone-like structures.

80. A: Long term energy storage in animals takes the form of fat. Animals also store energy as glycogen, and plants store energy as starch. , but these substances are for shorter-term use. Fats are a good storage form for chemical energy because fatty acids bond to glycerol in a condensation reaction to form fats (triglycerides). This reaction, which releases water, allows for the compacting of high-energy fatty acids in a concentrated form.

81. C: Plants exchange gases with the environment through pores in their leaves called stomata. Animals exchange gases with the environment in many different ways: small animals like flatworms exchange gases through their skin; insects use tracheae; and many species use lungs.

82. B: Carbon is released in the form of CO_2 through respiration, burning, and decomposition.

83. D: Most nitrogen is in the atmosphere in the form of N_2. In order for it to be used by living things, it must be fixed by nitrogen-fixing bacteria. These microorganisms convert N_2 to ammonia, which then forms NH_4^+ (ammonium).

84. B: The growth rate is equal to the difference between births and deaths divided by population size.

85. B: It is true that rocks are classified by their formation and the minerals they contain, while minerals are classified by their chemical composition and physical properties. Answer A is incorrect because rocks may contain traces of organic compounds. Answers C and D are incorrect because only minerals can be polymorphs and only rocks contain mineraloids.

86. D: Mineraloids are best defined as minerals that lack a crystalline structure, and they are typically found in rocks. Inorganic solids containing two or more minerals with different crystalline structures are known as polymorphs.

87. A: Chemical composition is not one of the physical properties used to classify minerals. The five major physical properties used to classify minerals are luster, hardness, cleavage, streak, and form. There is a separate classification system based on the chemical composition of minerals.

88. C: On Mohs scale of mineral hardness, talc has the lowest possible score (a one). Diamond is a ten, which is the highest possible score, and gypsum and fluorite have a score of two and four, respectively. Minerals can always scratch minerals that have a Mohs score lower than their own.

89. B: A mineral's true color is observed by conducting a streak test on unglazed porcelain tile. Paper is not appropriate for a streak test because it does not have the correct physical properties. External observation (inspecting the mineral's outer surface) is not sufficient to establish true color since streak tests sometimes reveal a color that is different from the substance's external hue. Finally, the luster test is not used to determine color.

90. A: The lithification process results in the formation of sedimentary rocks. During lithification, existing rock is compacted and liquid is squeezed from its pores. Eventually, the rock is cemented together, resulting in sedimentary rock.

91. C: Overgrazing and deforestation directly contribute to soil erosion by destroying the natural groundcover that normally prevents soil from being washed and blown away. These activities can ultimately result in desertification, which renders land unsuitable for agriculture.

92. C: Physical weathering of rocks can be caused by changes in temperature and pressure, as well as the freezing and thawing of water on the surfaces of rocks. Oxidation is a chemical process, not a physical one. Therefore, it is considered an example of chemical rather than physical weathering.

93. B: Plutonic, or intrusive, rock forms deep beneath the Earth's surface and cools slowly. Volcanic, or extrusive, rock solidifies at or near the surface. Hypabyssal rock forms below the Earth's surface, but not at a depth as great as plutonic rock. Detrital rock is a type of sedimentary rock.

94. B: Water is a key element in the lithification of sedimentary rock. After it is squeezed from the compressed material, it forms a chemical cement that holds the sedimentary rock in place. This cementation process is followed by recrystallization of the rock when equilibrium is reached.

95. B: Water that evaporates from oceans can precipitate over land due to the process of advection. Water vapor is less dense than air, and this difference in density produces convection currents that move the vapor, allowing it to condense and precipitate over land masses.

96. D: Water is likely to have the shortest residence time in the atmosphere. Water molecules linger in the atmosphere for an estimated 9 days, while their residence time in glaciers may range from 20 to 100 years. Water molecules reside in lakes for approximately 50 to 100 years, and they stay in rivers for two to six months.

97. D: In 1912, Alfred Wegener proposed that the continents once formed a single land mass called Pangaea, but have since drifted apart. Theories about the Earth's magnetic fields and plate tectonics did not emerge until years later. Once they did, they helped produce evidence to support Wegener's theory.

98. D: It is true that the ocean's salinity is usually between 34 and 35 parts per thousand, or 200 parts per million. Oceans comprise about 70.8 percent of the Earth's surface, and the ocean's deepest point is over 10,000 meters below sea level. The Mediterranean is considered a sea, not an ocean.

99. B: A guyot is defined as a seamount with a flattened top. The term "seamount" refers to any undersea volcano that is more than 1,000 meters tall. Undersea troughs are called trenches, and undersea mountain chains are called mid-ocean ridges.

100. B: Approximately 96.5 percent of seawater is comprised of hydrogen and oxygen. Although seawater does contain sodium, chlorine, magnesium, sulfur, and other dissolved solids, its primary components are the same substances that make up fresh water.

101. C: It is true that subsurface currents are driven by temperature and density variations, while surface currents are driven by wind. Ocean currents affect vast quantities of seawater and strongly influence the climate of Earth's landmasses.

102. B: It is true that the asthenosphere is hotter and more fluid than the lithosphere. The asthenosphere, also called the upper mantle, is the hot, fluid layer of the Earth's mantle upon which the lithosphere, or crust, is situated. Heat is transferred within the asthenosphere through a process called convection, which sometimes causes movement in the tectonic plates that make up the lithosphere.

103. A: The majority of weather phenomena occur in the Earth's troposphere. The troposphere is comprised of the area roughly 8-15 kilometers above the Earth's surface. It contains the majority of the mass of Earth's atmosphere and 99 percent of its water vapor.

104. A: According to the Köppen Climate Classification System, regions with continental climates are most commonly found in the interior regions of large landmasses. The continental climate is characterized by low levels of precipitation and large seasonal temperature variations.

105. C: Venus is not a gas giant. The four gas giants are Jupiter, Saturn, Uranus, and Neptune. While these "gas giants" are larger than Earth and are comprised mostly of gases, Venus is a terrestrial planet that is comparable in size to the Earth.

106. C: Sunlight consists of photons and cosmic rays. Sunlight is produces when hydrogen, deuterium, and tritium nuclei combine to form helium. This nuclear reaction is called fusion. Fission occurs when a nucleus disintegrates into two smaller nuclei. In both fission and fusion, energy is released because the binding energy per nucleon increases. This decreases the mass of the nuclei.

107. D: Expansion in the redshifts of galaxies, measurements of cosmic microwave background radiation, and measurements of the distribution of quasars and galaxies are all considered observational evidence in support of the Big Bang Theory. The abundance of certain "primordial elements" is also consistent with the theory.

108. A: Redshift is observed when a light-emitting object moves away from an observer. The observation of cosmological redshift supports the notion that the universe is expanding and the distance between Earth and far away galaxies is increasing. Redshift is an increase in the wavelength of light that appears visually as a movement toward the "red" end of the spectrum.

109. A: When students are taught science, the information needs to be correct, contextualized, and explained.

110. D: Prolonging the life of individuals in a current population will lead to an older age composition. An increased birth rate will cause population growth, but a greater proportion will be younger, not older.

111. D: With many species, factors like food, space, and predation have large effects on reproduction. Humans are able to control or at least affect many of these challenges, as well as the reproductive process itself, so other factors like education, religion, wealth, and access to health care are more significant factors in birth rates.

112. D: Air pollution would not be a direct result of clear-cutting forests. It would result in increased atmospheric CO_2, however, as well as localized climate change. Transpiration from trees in the tropical rain forest contributes largely to cloud formation and rain, so rainfall decreases because of clear-cutting, resulting in desertification.

113. B: When sulfur dioxide and nitrogen dioxide mix with water and other substances in the atmosphere, they produce sulfuric acid and nitric acid. These acids kill plants and animals when they reach the surface of the earth.

114. C: The main manmade cause of "dead zones" in portions of oceans and lakes that normally host abundant aquatic life is the use of chemical fertilizers. These fertilizers, which are high in nitrogen and phosphorous, enter lakes and rivers in water runoff and become concentrated in certain areas. This concentration, called eutrophication, eventually depletes the water's oxygen levels and renders it incapable of supporting life.

115. B: This question is asking about a concave MIRROR, not a lens. Since light does not pass through a mirror—it only reflects off of it—the different colors of light all bend the same amount. If light was passing through a lens, the different colors would bend slightly different amounts, causing chromatic aberration. That's not the case here. Spherical aberration occurs because the focal point of the mirror changes slightly as you move away from the center (optical axis). Astigmatism occurs when incident rays are not parallel to the optical axis. A circular beam, striking a lens or mirror at an angle to the optical axis, will become a parabola. Distortion concerns magnification and occurs in both mirrors and lenses.

116. A: A calorimeter is used to measure changes in heat. This instrument uses a thermometer to measure the amount of energy necessary to increase the temperature of water.

117. A: Commercial nuclear reactors generate electricity through the process of nuclear fission. The fission process is used to heat water, which in turn generates steam that is used to produce electricity. This process is controlled to ensure safety, but it does produce nuclear waste that requires the use of extensive procedures to dispose of it safely.

118. D: The Environmental Protection Agency (EPA) issues periodic reports on the condition of the nation's wetlands (areas that link land and water resources), watersheds (drainage basins where water, sediment and other material flows from a landmass into a body of water), and floodplains (a low area of land next to a body of water). One of the agency's missions is to preserve, protect, and maintain the quality of our water resources. They are accountable to the American people for the success or failure of their efforts.
The EPA is involved with various activities and works with other federal and state agencies, private industry, and environmental organizations to develop plans to protect the environment and manage water resources and the surrounding land by using a watershed protection approach. The EPA encourages integrated activities by:
   * Developing guidelines to link wetlands protection with watershed planning
   * Providing funding to the states for watershed projects
   * Integrating watershed projects into the federal floodplain plans
   * Supporting national and regional meetings to discuss wetlands and watershed planning
programs

119. D: According to information on the web site of the Environmental Protection Agency (EPA), treatment of hazardous waste is any process that changes the physical, chemical, or biological character of waste to make it less of an environmental threat. The treatment can neutralize the substance, recover energy or natural resources, make the substance less toxic, or prepare the waste for transport, storage, or disposal.
A common treatment method is incineration, which destroys the dangerous components in the substance and reduces the amount of waste. Sometimes the resulting ash may need additional treatment before it can be put in a landfill. The EPA has developed rigid standards for approved treatment options for specific types of hazardous waste. These options are defined in the Technology Codes and Description of Technology-Based Standards.

120. D: As is the case for many studies of human subjects, it is necessary to control for differences in behavior and genetics among the participants recruited into a study. In this case, it turned out that the real relationship to cancer was clear when study subjects were divided into smokers and nonsmokers. As it turns out, individuals that do not drink coffee are more likely to also abstain from smoking. Thus, coffee drinking nonsmokers do not have an increased risk of developing

cancer, while smokers, regardless of whether they drink caffeinated beverages, are more likely to develop cancers.

Practice Test #2

Practice Questions

1. Which of the following is needed for an experiment to be considered successful?
    a. a reasonable hypothesis
    b. a well-written lab report
    c. data that others can reproduce
    d. computer-aided statistical analysis

2. Which of the following is a characteristic of a reputable scientific journal?
    a. peer review of the quality of research
    b. famous scientists on the editorial board
    c. use of color graphics to represent data
    d. statistical analysis of all research data

3. Which of the following is the basic unit of volume in the metric system?
    a. kilogram
    b. liter
    c. meter
    d. centimeter

4. The measurement 0.0000043 meters, expressed correctly using scientific notation, is
    a. 4.3 m
    b. 4.3×10^{-7} m
    c. 4.3×10^{6} m
    d. 4.3×10^{-6} m

5. Which of the following conversion factors is a measured number?
    a. 12 in/ft
    b. 10 cm/dm
    c. 16 oz/lb
    d. 25 miles/gallon

6. What is the answer, with the correct number of significant figures, for this problem?
                4.392 grams + 102.40 grams + 2.51 grams =
    a. 110 grams
    b. 109 grams
    c. 109.302 grams
    d. 109.30 grams

7. The diagram below shows two batteries connected in series to a resistor. What is the direction of current flow?

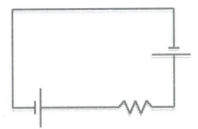

     a. clockwise
     b. counterclockwise
     c. neither clockwise nor counterclockwise
     d. Can't be determined from the information given.

Question 8: Consider the following information in answering the question which follows:

> A class exercise involves demonstration of the principle of neutralization of acids and bases. The reagents available are 1 M NaOH, concentrated HCl, water, and phenol red [a pH indicator that turns from yellow to red under basic conditions]. The procedure chosen by the teacher is as follows:
> *Step 1*: Prior to class, the teacher prepares 1 M HCl by adding 914 ml water to 86 ml of HCl. [Note that concentrated HCl is 11.65 M.]
> *Step 2*: Since the class is divided into nine groups of three students, the teacher distributes the 1 M HCl into nine 125 ml flasks.
> *Step 3*: Each group is given a dropper bottle with phenol red, a bottle containing 200 ml of 1 M NaOH, and a 25 ml pipette with bulb.
> *Step 4*: The students are instructed to add the phenol red to the HCl until a visible yellow color is seen, record the color, then slowly add NaOH, and record the volume of NaOH required to make the solution alkaline.

8. What change would have to be made to this procedure to allow the students to complete the experiment and see the solution become neutralized?
     a. The students should use 10 M NaOH so the titration is more rapid.
     b. The HCl should be distributed in 250 ml flasks.
     c. The students should alternate addition of NaOH and phenol red.
     d. The NaOH should be added using a dropper bottle.

9. Random error could be caused by which of the following problems?
     a. Imperfectly calibrated equipment
     b. Extraneous disturbances that cannot be controlled
     c. Consistent human error in the use of lab equipment
     d. Failure to account for a specific variable

10. What information is contained in the safety icon below?

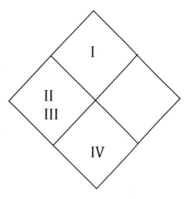

    a. I = name of chemical, II = chemical formula, III = structural formula, IV = molecular weight
    b. I = # of protons, II = # of neutrons, III = # of electrons, IV = atomic weight
    c. I = chemical safety, II = biological safety, III = radiation safety, IV = emergency preparedness
    d. I = health, II = flammability, III = reactivity, IV = protective equipment

11. What is the chronological order in which the following significant events occurred in the history of science?

I.   the idea of an atom as the smallest unit of matter
II. synthesis of an organic molecule in the laboratory
III. discovery of the structure of DNA
IV. principle of distillation
V. discovery of oxygen

    a. I, II, III, IV, V
    b. I, V, IV, II, III
    c. IV, V, I, II, III
    d. IV, I, V, II, III

12. Which of the following pairs of a person and an accomplishment is NOT correct?
    a. Lavoisier, concept that water is formed from oxygen and hydrogen
    b. Mendeleev, the periodic table
    c. Volta, discovery of the battery
    d. Einstein, synthesis of the first man-made element

13. Which of the following is a characteristic of nonmetals?
    a. good conductors of electricity
    b. malleable
    c. shiny
    d. low melting points

14. Which of the following elements is a noble gas?
    a. nitrogen
    b. bromine
    c. oxygen
    d. argon

15. The electron arrangement of any particular atom shows
    a. the number of isotopes possible.
    b. a diagram of the atomic nucleus.
    c. the maximum number of electrons each energy level can hold.
    d. the number of electrons in each energy level.

16. The octet rule indicates that
    a. all of the Group A elements have eight valence electrons.
    b. the noble gases react with other compounds to get eight valence electrons.
    c. all of the shells in an atom hold a maximum of eight electrons.
    d. atoms lose, gain, or share valence electrons to have eight valence electrons.

17. In an atom, the nucleus contains
    a. all the protons and electrons.
    b. only protons.
    c. an equal number of protons and electrons.
    d. all the protons and neutrons.

18. The number of neutrons in an atom is equal to
    a. the mass number.
    b. the mass number minus the atomic number.
    c. the mass number plus the atomic number.
    d. the number of protons.

19. Which of the following is an example of nuclear fission?
    a. the formation of helium in our sun
    b. the atomic bombs used at the end of WWII
    c. the hydrogen bombs tested during the Cold War
    d. particles created in the Large Hadron Collider (LHC)

20. In a nuclear chain reaction which of the following occurs?
    a. Electrons are emitted by each split nucleus generating heat.
    b. Released electrons are captured by other nuclei.
    c. When a nucleus is split by a neutron, it releases an additional neutron.
    d. Electrons become excited and move to higher energy levels.

21. The minimum weight of fissionable isotope necessary for a fission reaction to maintain itself is
    a. the critical mass.
    b. always one mole.
    c. inversely proportional to the atomic weight of the isotope.
    d. calculated by multiplying the atomic weight of the isotope by Planck's constant.

22. The specific heat of aluminum is 0.215 cal/g°C. How much energy is required to change the temperature of 10 grams of aluminum from 25°C to 75°C?
   a. 10.04 cal
   b. 51.29 cal
   c. 107.5 cal
   d. 118.6 cal

23. If the reaction shown below is exothermic, the energy level of the reactants is
$$H_2 + O_2 \rightarrow 2\ H_2O$$
   a. lower than that of the products.
   b. higher than the activation energy of the reaction.
   c. the same as that of the products.
   d. higher than that of the products.

24. Any reaction that absorbs 150 kcal of energy can be classified as
   a. activated.
   b. exothermic.
   c. reduction.
   d. endothermic.

25. Which of the following is a characteristic of the modern periodic table?
   a. The A groups contain the transition elements.
   b. A group is a horizontal row on the periodic table.
   c. A period is a column on the periodic table.
   d. The elements in each group have similar chemical properties.

26. The elements lithium, sodium, and potassium
   a. are in the same period of elements.
   b. are in the same group.
   c. have the same mass number.
   d. are isotopes of one another.

27. Elements in group IIA(2) of the periodic table form ions with a charge of
   a. 0
   b. 1⁻
   c. 2⁺
   d. 1⁺

28. Which of the following is a physical change?
   a. fermenting grapes to produce wine
   b. dry ice subliming
   c. baking a cake
   d. digesting a meal

29. How many protons are in an isotope of sodium with a mass number of 25?
   a. 11
   b. 14
   c. 15
   d. 32

30. Isotopes are atoms of the same element that have
    a. the same atomic number but different numbers of protons.
    b. the same atomic mass but different numbers of protons.
    c. the same atomic number but different numbers of electrons.
    d. the same atomic number but different numbers of neutrons.

31. Hydrochloric acid and calcium carbonate react according to this balanced chemical reaction:
$$2HCl + 1CaCO_3 \rightarrow 1CaCl_2 + 1CO_2 + 1H_2O$$
What volume of carbon dioxide (CO_2) gas is produced when this reaction goes to completion at standard temperature and pressure?
    a. 1 liter
    b. 1 mole
    c. 3 liters
    d. 22.4 liters

32. What elements are in hydroxyapatite, $Ca_5(PO_4)_3OH$, a major compound in human bones and teeth?
    a. calcium, phosphorus, oxygen, hydrogen
    b. carbon, potassium, oxygen, helium
    c. carbon, potassium, oxygen, hydrogen
    d. calcium, phosphorus, oxygen, helium

33. Which element will most likely form a covalently bonded compound when it bonds with sulfur?
    a. argon (Ar)
    b. iron (Fe)
    c. lithium (Li)
    d. oxygen (O)

34. When heat is removed from water during condensation, new ____ form.
    a. atoms
    b. covalent bonds
    c. intermolecular bonds
    d. ionic bonds

35. Which of the following compounds contains an ionic bond?
    a. H_2O
    b. H_2
    c. CaO
    d. CH_4

36. What is the percent composition of each element in $C_6H_{12}O_6$?
    a. 6% carbon; 12% hydrogen; 6% oxygen
    b. 25% carbon; 50% hydrogen; 25% oxygen
    c. 40% carbon; 6.7% hydrogen; 53.5% oxygen
    d. 37.5% carbon; 12.5% hydrogen; 50% oxygen

37. How many moles of K_2SO_4 are in 15.0 grams of K_2SO_4?
    a. 0.0861 moles
    b. 2.61 x 10³ moles
    c. 0.119 moles
    d. 0.172 moles

38. In terms of mass, which of the following represents the greatest amount of sucrose (Molar mass = 342 grams)?
    a. 1 mole
    b. 100 grams
    c. 1 L of a 0.1 M solution
    d. 100 mL of a 1 M solution

39. Which of the following is an example of an oxidation-reduction reaction?
    a. A volcano eruption can be modeled using vinegar and baking soda.
    b. Steel cans are electroplated with tin to produce grocery store food cans.
    c. Blood catalyzes the decomposition of hydrogen peroxide on a cut.
    d. Bread dough rises from the production of carbon dioxide gas by yeast.

40. Which of the following conditions and ion pairs is an example of a buffer?
    a. homeostasis; carbonic acid / bicarbonate ion
    b. water has a neutral pH; hydronium / hydroxide
    c. copper can be electroplated onto tin; Cu^+ / Sn^{+2}
    d. aluminum hydroxide is not soluble; Al^{+3} / OH^-

41. A solution is made by dissolving 87.75 grams of NaCl into 500 mL of water. What is the weight percent of the NaCl in the solution?
    a. 2%
    b. 5.69%
    c. 14.93%
    d. 17.55%

42. According to the solubility curves below, the solubility of which substance is *least* affected by a temperature change?

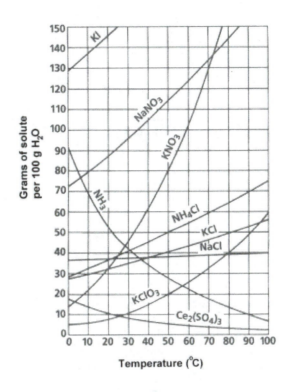

a. KI
b. NH₃
c. KNO₃
d. NaCl

43. Which of the following measurements has the most significant digits?
    a. 0.2990
    b. 2.9900
    c. 2.997
    d. 0.00209

44. Consider the following statements about Newton's law:
I. A Newton is a fundamental unit.
II. Mass and acceleration are inversely related when the force is constant.
III. Newton's first law can be derived from Newton's second law.
IV. Newton's second law can be derived from the universal law of gravity.
Which of the following statements are true?
    a. I, II, and III.
    b. II and III only.
    c. III only.
    d. I, II, III, and IV are not true.

The information below pertains to question 45:

Mass of moon (M_m)	$(7.36 \times 10^{22})\ kg$
Mass of earth (M_e)	$5.9742 \times 10^{24}\ kg$
Gravitational constant (G)	$(6.67 \times 10^{-11})\ \dfrac{N - m^2}{kg^2}$
Distance between earth and the moon (d)	$3.84 \times 10^3\ km$
Force of gravity on Earth (g)	$9.81\ m/s^2$

45. Use the information in the table above to identify the mathematical expression that could be used to correctly calculate the force of gravity in Newtons between Earth and its moon.

a. $F = \dfrac{(6.67 \times 10^{-11}) \times (7.36 \times 10^{22}) \times (5.9742 \times 10^{24})}{3.84 \times 10^3}$

b. $F = \dfrac{(9.81) \times (7.36 \times 10^{22}) \times (5.9742 \times 10^{24})}{3.84 \times 10^3}$

c. $F = \dfrac{(6.67 \times 10^{-11}) \times (3.84 \times 10^3)}{(7.36 \times 10^{22}) \times (5.9742 \times 10^{24})}$

d. $F = \dfrac{(6.67 \times 10^{-11}) \times (7.36 \times 10^{22}) \times (5.9742 \times 10^{24})}{(9.81) \times (3.84 \times 10^3)}$

46. 10 N of force are exerted on a sphere at an angle of 30°. An additional 10 N of force are exerted at an angle of 210°. Which statement about the sphere is correct?
    a. The sphere is in a state of equilibrium and not moving.
    b. The sphere is in a state of accelerating velocity.
    c. The sphere is moving along a line at a 120° angle.
    d. The sphere is experiencing additional g-force.

47. A pulley lifts a 1 kg object 10 m into the air in 5 seconds. How much work is done?
    a. 10 J
    b. 10 W
    c. 98.1 N
    d. 98.1 J

48. A pulley lifts a 5 kg object 10 m into the air in 5 seconds. How much power is used?
    a. 50 J
    b. 50 N
    c. 98.1 J
    d. 98.1 W

49. The ideal mechanical advantage (IMA) of a pulley system indicates how much force is required to lift a mass. A fixed puley has an IMA of 1 because all it only changes the direction of the force. A floating pulley has an IMA of 2. The total IMA is the product of the individual pulleys' IMAs. What is the ideal mechanical advantage of the pulley system below?

a. 1
b. 2
c. 3
d. 4

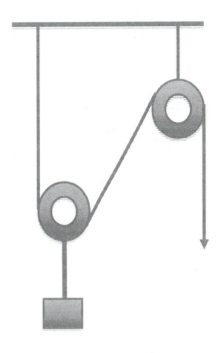

50. Which of the following statements about a solid metal sphere with a net charge is true?
    a. If the charge is positive it will be distributed uniformly throughout the sphere.
    b. The charge will be distributed uniformly at the surface of the sphere.
    c. The charge will leave the sphere.
    d. The electric field will be tangent to the surface of the sphere.

51. What does it mean when someone says that electric charge is conserved?
    a. Like charges repel, and unlike charges attract.
    b. The net charge of an isolated system remains constant.
    c. Charges come from electrons and protons.
    d. Charge can never be created or destroyed.

52. An electron moves in a uniform electric field in the same direction as the electric field from point A to point B. Which of the following statements is true?
    a. The potential energy of the electron decreased
    b. The potential energy of the electron
    c. The potential energy of the electron remained constant
    d. The potential energy of the electron was converted into kinetic energy

53. Which of the following creates an electromagnet?
    a. rapidly spinning and rotating electrons inside an iron bar
    b. an iron bar moving inside a coil of wire that contains a current
    c. the movement of electrons through a complete circuit
    d. convection currents within the liquid core of Earth's interior

54. What wave characteristic determines if visible light is red or blue?
    a. frequency
    b. amplitude
    c. wavelength
    d. speed of sound

55. The two waves shown below meet.

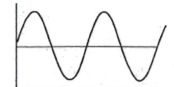

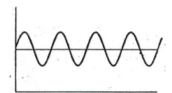

What is the shape of the resulting wave?

a.

b.

c.

d.

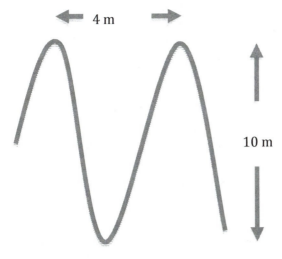

4 m

10 m

56. What is the wavelength in the above diagram?
    a. 2 meters
    b. 4 meters
    c. 5 meters
    d. 10 meters

57. Which of the following statements best explains why light is polarized?
    a. Light waves' electromagnetic fields can be oriented in a particular direction by a polarizer.
    b. Photons of light can be pointed in the same direction by microscopic holes in a polarizer.
    c. Light travels in a vacuum.
    d. Light is a longitudinal wave.

58. What corresponds to the amplitude of a sound wave?
    a. loudness
    b. pressure differential of fluctuations
    c. magnitude of motion of air molecules
    d. power

59. What property of a sound wave in air corresponds to the frequency of the sound?
    a. pitch
    b. high and low
    c. timbre
    d. overtones

60. In musical instruments with two open ends, the first harmonic fits one-half wave inside the tube. The second harmonic fits 1 full wave in the tube. The third harmonic fits 1.5 full waves in the tube. Etc. An organ pipe, open at both ends, has a length of 1.2 meters. What is the frequency of the third harmonic? The speed of sound is 340 meters per second.
    a. 142 Hz
    b. 284 Hz
    c. 425 Hz
    d. 568 Hz

61. Which of the following cell types has a peptidoglycan cell wall?
   a. Algae
   b. Bacteria
   c. Fungi
   d. Land plants

62. Which of the following statements regarding chemiosmosis in mitochondria is not correct?
   a. ATP synthase is powered by protons flowing through membrane channels
   b. Energy from ATP is used to transport protons to the intermembrane space
   c. Energy from the electron transport chain is used to transport protons to the intermembrane space
   d. An electrical gradient and a pH gradient both exist across the inner membrane

63. All of the following are examples ways of controlling eukaryotic gene expression EXCEPT
   a. Nucleosome packing
   b. Methylation of DNA
   c. RNA interference
   d. Operons

64. Transfer of DNA between bacteria using a narrow tube called a pilus is called
   a. Transformation
   b. Transduction
   c. Operation
   d. Conjugation

65. The synaptonemal complex is present in which of the following phases of the cell cycle?
   a. Metaphase of meiosis I
   b. Telophase of meiosis I
   c. Metaphase of meiosis II
   d. Telophase of meiosis II

66. In DNA replication, which of the following enzymes is required for separating the DNA molecule into two strands?
   a. DNA polymerase
   b. Single strand binding protein
   c. DNA gyrase
   d. Helicase

67. Which of the following kinds of plants is most likely to perform CAM photosynthesis?
   a. Mosses
   b. Grasses
   c. Deciduous trees
   d. Cacti

68. The combination of DNA with histones is called
   a. A centromere
   b. Chromatin
   c. A chromatid
   d. Nucleoli

69. Which of the following is true of the enzyme telomerase?
    a. It is active on the leading strand during DNA synthesis
    b. It requires a chromosomal DNA template
    c. It acts in the 3′ → 5′ direction
    d. It adds a repetitive DNA sequence to the end of chromosomes

70. Substrate for DNA ligase
    a. Okazaki fragments
    b. RNA primer
    c. Single-strand binding protein
    d. Leading strand

71. Which of the following mutations is most likely to have a dramatic effect on the sequence of a protein?
    a. A point mutation
    b. A missense mutation
    c. A deletion
    d. A silent mutation

72. Which of the following could be an end product of transcription?
    a. rRNA
    b. DNA
    c. Protein
    d. snRNP

73. In ferns, the joining of egg and sperm produces a zygote, which will grow into the
    a. Gametophyte
    b. Sporophyte
    c. Spore
    d. Sporangium

74. Which of the following would create the greatest amount of genetic variation for a diploid species in a single generation?
    a. Crossing over
    b. Mutation
    c. Hybridization
    d. Independent assortment of homologs

75. Darwin's idea that evolution occurs by the gradual accumulation of small changes can be summarized as
    a. Punctuated equilibrium
    b. Phyletic gradualism
    c. Convergent evolution
    d. Adaptive radiation

76. Which of the following processes of speciation would most likely occur if a species of bird were introduced into a group of islands that were previously uninhabited by animals?
    a. Allopatric speciation
    b. Adaptive radiation
    c. Sympatric speciation
    d. Artificial speciation

77. In the food chain above, vultures represent
    a. Scavengers
    b. Detritivores
    c. Primary carnivores
    d. Herbivores

78. Which of the following plant structures allows for gas exchange?
    a. Phloem
    b. Cuticle
    c. Meristem
    d. Stomata

79. Leaves have parallel veins
    a. Monocots
    b. Dicots
    c. Angiosperms
    d. Gymnosperms

80. Which of the following blood components is involved in blood clotting?
    a. Red blood cells
    b. Platelets
    c. White blood cells
    d. Leukocytes

81. Which section of the digestive system is responsible for water reabsorption?
    a. The large intestine
    b. The duodenum
    c. The small intestine
    d. The stomach

82. Which of the following habitats would provide an opportunity for secondary succession?
    a. A retreating glacier
    b. Burned cropland
    c. A newly formed volcanic island
    d. A 500 year old forest

83. Which biome is most likely to support the growth of epiphytes?
    a. Deserts
    b. Tropical rain forests
    c. Temperate deciduous forests
    d. Taigas

84. When a population reaches its carrying capacity
    a. Other populations will be forced out of the habitat
    b. Density-dependent factors no longer play a role
    c. Density-independent factors no longer play a role
    d. The population growth rate approaches zero

85. A mineral's true color is observed by:
    a. Conducting a streak test on white paper.
    b. Conducting a streak test on unglazed porcelain tile.
    c. Inspecting the mineral's outer surface.
    d. Shining a light on the mineral to inspect its luster.

86. Galena, pyrite, and magnetite are examples of minerals with which of the following types of luster?
    a. Pearly
    b. Greasy
    c. Adamantine
    d. Metallic

87. According to the Dana classification system, gold, silver, and copper belong to which class?
    a. Organic
    b. Elemental
    c. Oxide
    d. Sulfide

88. According to the Dana classification system, minerals that contain the anion SO_4^{2-} are part of which chemical class?
    a. Sulfate
    b. Sulfite
    c. Halide
    d. Phosphate

89. Minerals that form on the sea floor from discarded shells are most likely part of which chemical class?
    a. Sulfate
    b. Organic
    c. Carbonate
    d. Silicate

90. Which of the following is NOT an example of chemical weathering of rocks?
    a. Highly acidic rainwater causes dissolution of rocks.
    b. Minerals that comprise rocks take on water, causing them to enlarge and creating fractures within the rocks.
    c. Salt water penetrates fractures in rocks and leaves behind salt crystals that cause fractures.
    d. Iron molecules in rocks react with atmospheric oxygen, which causes oxidation.

91. Which of the following lists places several phases of the sedimentary cycle in the correct order?
    a. Erosion, weathering, transportation, deposition
    b. Weathering, erosion, deposition, transportation
    c. Weathering, deposition, erosion, transportation
    d. Weathering, erosion, transportation, deposition

92. Nondetrital sedimentary rock is produced by:
    a. Chemical precipitation.
    b. Cooling of magma just below the Earth's surface.
    c. Physical weathering processes.
    d. Weathering of igneous rock.

93. Which of the following statements is true of rocks such as olivine that are found at the top of Bowen's reaction series?
    a. They are classified as metamorphic.
    b. They weather more quickly than rocks found lower in the series.
    c. They crystallize at lower temperatures than rocks found at the bottom of the series.
    d. None of the above

94. The mountain in Figure 1 has the oldest rock in its core and the youngest rock in its outer layers. Which of the following terms best describes the mountain?
    a. Syncline
    b. Anticline
    c. Fault-block
    d. Graben

Figure 1.

95. When fault-block mountains like those in the Western United States are formed, sections that are lifted by tensional forces are called:
    a. Antiforms.
    b. Faces.
    c. Horsts.
    d. Rifts.

96. When water changes directly from a solid to a gas, skipping the liquid state, this is called:
    a. Evapotranspiration.
    b. Condensation.
    c. Sublimation.
    d. Runoff.

97. The Cretaceous-Tertiary Event, during which non-avian dinosaurs became extinct, occurred approximately how long ago?
    a. 10,000 years ago
    b. 15.5 million years ago
    c. 38 million years ago
    d. 65.5 million years ago

98. The Coriolis effect in the Earth's oceans is caused by:
    a. The Earth's rotation.
    b. The Earth's magnetic field.
    c. Variations in the density of seawater.
    d. The Gulf Stream.

99. Thermohaline circulation is caused by:
    a. Temperature differences between seawater only.
    b. Salinity differences between seawater only.
    c. Variations in seawater density caused by both temperature and salinity differences.
    d. None of the above

100. When cold, nutrient-rich water is allowed to rise to the surface because winds parallel to a landmass's coast blow the surface water towards the open sea, this is called:
    a. Ekman transport.
    b. The Coriolis effect.
    c. Upwelling.
    d. Downwelling.

101. The frequency of ocean waves is measured by:
    a. The distance between a wave's crest and trough.
    b. The distance between the crests of two subsequent waves.
    c. The time between two subsequent wave crests.
    d. The number of wave crests that pass a given point each second.

102. The majority of the solar energy that reaches Earth is absorbed by:
    a. Glaciers.
    b. Landmasses.
    c. Oceans.
    d. The Earth's atmosphere.

103. Air is a(n)
    a. homogeneous mixture.
    b. element.
    c. heterogeneous mixture.
    d. compound.

104. Tropical climate zones are characterized by:
    a. Extreme temperature variations between night and day.
    b. Extreme temperature variations between seasons.
    c. Frequent rainfall.
    d. All of the above

105. The asteroid belt in our solar system is located between:
    a. Earth and Mars.
    b. Neptune and Pluto.
    c. Uranus and Saturn.
    d. Mars and Jupiter.

106. The distance from the Earth to the Sun is equal to one:
    a. Astronomical unit.
    b. Light year.
    c. Parsec.
    d. Arcsecond.

107. Which of the following statements best describes the physical structure of the universe?
    a. Galaxies are the largest structures in the universe, and they are distributed evenly throughout space.
    b. Superclusters are the largest structures in the universe, and they are distributed evenly throughout space.
    c. Superclusters are the largest structures in the universe, and they are unevenly distributed so that large voids exist in space.
    d. Filaments are the largest structures in the universe, and they surround large, bubble-like voids.

108. The Hertzsprung-Russell (H-R) Diagram is used primarily to:
    a. Determine a star's age by comparing its temperature and luminosity.
    b. Measure a star's size by estimating its luminosity.
    c. Determine a galaxy's luminosity when its size is known.
    d. Group galaxies by their morphological types.

109. During primary succession, which species would most likely be a pioneer species?
    a. Lichens
    b. Fir trees
    c. Mosquitoes
    d. Dragonflies

110. Which of the following is NOT a natural dispersal process that would lead to species colonization on an island?
    a. Mussels carried into a lake on the hull of a ship
    b. Drought connecting an island to other land
    c. Floating seeds
    d. Animals swimming long distances

111. Genetic engineering
    a. Involves introducing new proteins to a cell
    b. Involves transient expression of genes
    c. Can have no environmental affects
    d. Requires using restriction enzymes to cut DNA

112. Which of the following would most likely be disruptive to the flowering time of a day-neutral plant?
    a. Daylight interrupted by a brief dark period
    b. Daylight interrupted by a long dark period
    c. High daytime temperatures
    d. Night interrupted by a brief exposure to red light

113. Which of the following organisms would be most likely to have mercury in their bodies?
    a. Mosquitoes
    b. Frogs
    c. Filter-feeding fish
    d. Fish-eating birds

114. Which of the following is not a responsibility of the U.S. Army Corp of Engineers?
    a. Dams and dikes
    b. Hazardous waste
    c. Construction of artificial islands
    d. Permits for waterway-related activities

115. Environmental scientists study:
    a. the quality of the natural environment
    b. the predicted impact of human activity
    c. strategies developed to restore ecosystems
    d. All of the above

116. Which of the following activities is not a responsibility of the Food and Drug Administration?
    a. Testing products
    b. Ensure the safety of food
    c. Ban marketing and distribution of certain products
    d. Review data from clinical trials

117. What is standard temperature and pressure?
    a. the conditions under which water freezes
    b. 0° C and 1 atmosphere pressure
    c. 25° C and 1 atmosphere pressure
    d. 0° C and 1 pound per square inch

118. High-boiling liquids should be distilled under reduced pressure because
    a. they have high vapor pressures
    b. they have low melting points
    c. they can decompose at temperatures below their boiling points
    d. they do not boil at normal pressure

119. Colored impurities can often be removed from a compound during the recrystallization process by
    a. filtration
    b. addition of a cosolvent
    c. addition of activated charcoal powder
    d. chromatography

120. Chromatography is a method of purifying compounds that depends on
    a. solubility
    b. absorption
    c. adsorption/desorption equilibria
    d. polarity

Answers and Explanations

1. C: For an experiment to be considered successful, it must yield data that others can reproduce. Answer choice a may be considered part of a well-designed experiment. Answer choices b, d, and e may be considered part of an experiment that is reported on by individuals with expertise.

2. A: A characteristic of a reputable scientific journal is that there is peer review of the quality of the research. Others may be characteristics of scientific journals, but these do not necessarily mean a journal is reputable.

3. B: Kilograms and grams are units of mass, while centimeters and meters are units of length.

4. D: Self-explanatory.

5. D: To determine miles per gallon, one must measure the distance traveled per quantity of fuel. The other factors provided are conversions between and within systems of measurement or defined quantities, such as 12 being equal to a dozen.

6. D: The number of significant figures in a calculation is equivalent to the quantity with the fewest significant figures. In this case, two of the quantities have two significant figures to the right of the decimal, so the sum must also have the same number of significant figures to the right of the decimal.

7. D: Conventional current is the flow of positive charges from the positive to negative sides of a battery. In reality, protons do not move through a wire. Rather, negatively charged electrons move through the wire, so conventional current reflects the effective motion of positive charge created by electrons moving in the opposite direction. Normally, the wide side of the battery represents the positive side, so conventional current would start from the wide side and move around until it reached the narrow side of the battery. Here the batteries aren't labeled with positive or negative, but since the batteries are oriented in opposite directions, that does not matter. If they had the same exact voltage, no current would flow. However, if one battery has a higher voltage than the other, the higher voltage battery would dominate the direction of current flow. Since the voltage of the batteries is unknown, the direction of current flow cannot be determined.

8. B: Neutralization of 100 ml of 1 M HCl with 1 M NaOH will require the addition of 100 ml of NaOH. The final volume of solution would be 200 ml, requiring a container with a volume greater than 125 ml.

9. B: Random error could be caused by extraneous disturbances that cannot be controlled. Random error is that which does not affect experimental results in a consistent, patterned way. In contrast, systematic error affects all experimental results consistently. For example, if an instrument is calibrated improperly, all experimental results will be skewed in the same direction.

10. D: The information contained in the safety icon is as follows: I = health, II = flammability, III = reactivity, and IV = protective equipment.

11. D: Distillation of alcohol for consumption was known at least as early as 2000 BC. The Greek philosophers Democritus and Leucippus proposed the idea of atoms around 400 BC. Joseph

Priestley discovered oxygen in 1774. Frederick Wohler synthesized urea in his laboratory in 1828. Watson and Crick reported the structure of DNA in 1953.

12. D: While there is an element, Einsteinium (symbol Es), named after Albert Einstein, he was not a chemist.

13. D: Nonmetals generally have relatively low melting points, are brittle, and are poor conductors of heat and electricity.

14. D: Noble gases are the group VIIIA elements, which have full outer electron shells and thus do not have any valence electrons. Since they do not associate with other elements, they have been termed noble.

15. D: The electron arrangement for an atom does not provide any direct information concerning the nucleus or the possible number of stable isotopes. It provides the number of electrons which occupy each energy level of that particular atom but does not include information as to the shape of the electron shells nor the number of possible electron configurations for other atoms.

16. D: The octet rule can also be restated to say that all atoms gain and lose electrons to achieve a noble gas configuration, where the highest occupied energy level (electron shell) is fully occupied with eight, or a multiple of eight, electrons.

17. D: The nucleus is comprised of neutrons and protons. While atoms generally have an equal number of electrons and protons, electrons are not a component of the nucleus.

18. B: The atomic number of an element corresponds to the number of protons in the nucleus. The mass number is the number of protons plus the number of neutrons, i.e. the sum of the subatomic particles that have any appreciable mass.

19. B: The only example of nuclear fission is answer choice b. The nuclear reaction in the stars, including our sun (a), is a nuclear fusion reaction. Hydrogen bombs (c) are also examples of nuclear fusion. The Large Hadron Collider (d) does not operate by means of nuclear reactions.

20. C: Nuclear fission generally involves the bombardment of a fissible isotope, such as ^{235}U, with neutrons. Each atom that is split by a neutron also liberates at least one additional neutron. Thus, each nuclear fission event yields at least two neutrons, which can each cause more fission events, propagating a chain reaction.

21. A: Nuclear fission reactions require a sufficient amount of the fissionable isotope so that neutrons liberated by fission events are likely to encounter additional atoms of the fissionable isotope. The quantity of material necessary to fulfill this criterion is termed the critical mass and varies depending on the element and concentration of the fissionable isotope present in the material to be used to sustain the reaction.

22. C: The formula used to answer this problem is $Q = mc\Delta T$. Using the values provided in the question, $Q = (10g) \times (0.215 \text{ cal/g°C}) \times (50°C)$. Therefore, $Q = 107.5$ cal.
Answer a used the following incorrect formula: $Q = (m \times c) / \Delta T$.
Answer b used the following incorrect formula: $Q = (c \times \Delta T) / m$.
Answer d incorrectly applied the concept of (1 food calorie = 1Kcal). Therefore, incorrect units were used.

23. D: In an exothermic reaction, heat is generated when the reactants give rise to product. In such reactions, the reactants have a higher energy level. The energy released, or the heat of reaction, corresponds to the difference in energy level between the reactants and the reaction products.

24. D: Reactions that require energy are termed endothermic, as opposed to those where the reaction generates heat and are designated exothermic. These terms refer solely to the heat of reaction and not the mechanism of the reaction.

25. D: The periodic table is organized to group together, in the same column, elements which have similar chemical properties. By inspection, a review of the periodic table shows that transition elements are the "B" group elements, each period is a row representing a series of elements with increasing atomic numbers, and the representative elements include all the groups except the transition elements.

26. B: Lithium, sodium, and potassium are alkali metals (Group IA). They are neither in the same period (row) nor do they share a common mass or number of neutrons and, as such, are not isotopes of each other.

27. C: Elements in Group IIA have two electrons in the highest energy level. For example, beryllium (Be), with an atomic number of 4, has two electrons in the first energy level and two in the second, leaving that shell only partially filled with room for six additional electrons. Similarly, magnesium (Mg) with an atomic number of 12 has the occupied energy levels containing two, eight, and two electrons. Again, the highest energy level is unfilled by six electrons. Therefore, to form an ion, the Group IIA elements lose two electrons, rather than gain six, to achieve a net charge of 2^+.

28. B: The sublimation of dry ice, that is the transition directly from a solid to a gas, represents a change in the physical state of carbon dioxide. No chemical bonds are broken or formed in the process. In contrast, fermentation (conversion of sugar to alcohol), baking, digestion of food, and a tomato ripening all involve one or more changes in the chemical composition of a complex mixture.

29. A: The mass number of an element is defined as the number of protons (atomic number) plus the number of neutrons in the nucleus. The atomic number of sodium is 11, so there are 11 protons in the nucleus of all isotopes of sodium. In this case, where the mass number is 25, there must be 14 neutrons (25 − 11) in the isotope of sodium.

30. D: All atoms of the same element have the same number of protons and, thus, have the same atomic number. Isotopes of an element differ in the number of neutrons present in the nucleus. This means that isotopes of an element all have the same atomic number, but the mass number differs as a function of the number of neutrons.

31. D: According to the balanced equation, 1 mole of carbon dioxide gas is produced. At the standard temperature and pressure conditions for the stated reaction, one mole of gas occupies 22.4 liters.

32. A: Self-explanatory; see the periodic table.

33. D: Covalent bonds form when two non-metals bond. Oxygen is the only non-metal in the answer choices. Iron (Fe) is a transition metal. Lithium (Li) is an alkali metal. Argon is a noble gas and does not react with other elements.

34. C: A physical change occurs when water condenses. The only thing formed during condensation is new intermolecular bonds. Therefore, no new covalent bonds form (b). The only time new atoms form is during a nuclear reaction (a). The water molecule is not ionizing, so no new ionic bonds form (d).

35. C: Ionic bonds generally involve metals and nonmetals and involve one element losing its valence electrons to the other. In general, elements that are close together on the periodic table are more likely to share valence electrons and form covalent bonds.

36. C: The percent composition of each element in $C_6H_{12}O_6$ is 40% carbon, 6.7% hydrogen, and 53.5% oxygen.
Answer choice a is incorrect because it simply converts the subscripts to a percent.
Answer choice b is incorrect because it looks at the number of atoms in the molecule instead of the mass of each element in the molecule.
Answer choice d is incorrect because the percent is based on the atomic number of each element instead of the atomic mass.

37. A: To determine the number of moles of K_2SO_4 in 15.0 grams, the molecular weight of the substance must be calculated. The molecular weight (MW) is the sum of the atomic weights (AW) of the atoms in the molecule, as shown in the following table:

atom	AW	# of atoms/molecule	contribution to MW
K	39.1	2	78.2
S	32.1	1	32.1
O	16.0	4	64.0
total			174.3

Having determined that the MW of K_2SO_4 is 174.3 g/mole. We can calculate the number of moles of the compound in 15.0 grams as follows:

$$15.0 \text{ g} /174.3 \text{ g mole}^{-1} = 15.0 \text{ g} /174.3 \text{ g mole}^{-1} =$$
$$15.0/174.3 \text{ moles} = 0.0861 \text{ moles}$$

38. A: Since the molar mass of sucrose is 342 grams, one mole weighs 342 grams. This is greater than 100 grams b. In one liter of a 0.1 M solution c. there are 34.2 grams of sucrose. (1 ~~liter~~*0.1 moles/~~liter~~ = 0.1 moles; 0.1 ~~moles~~*342 grams/~~mole~~ = 34.2 grams) In 100 ml (0.1 liters) of a 1 M solution d. , there are 34.2 grams of sucrose. (0.1 ~~liter~~*1 moles/~~liter~~ = 0.1 moles; 0.1 ~~moles~~*342 grams/~~mole~~ = 34.2 grams)

39. B: Tin cans are steel cans with a tin coating. Applying this coating involves an oxidation-reduction reaction. Choice a is a double replacement reaction. Choices c and d are decomposition reactions.

40. A: The condition and ion pair is an example of a buffer. Choice b refers to pH. Choice c refers to redox reactions and the activity series. Choice d refers to solubility rules.

41. C: Weight percent is calculated using the following mathematical expression:

Weight percent = (mass of component / total mass of solution) x 100. Therefore, (87.75/587.75) x 100 = 14.93%.
Answer choice a is incorrect because the mass of NaCl was first converted to moles and then divided by 0.5L.
Answer choice b is incorrect because the mass of the water in the solution was divided by the mass of the NaCl.
Answer choice d is incorrect because the mass of the NaCl was divided by the mass of the water, not the total mass of the solution.

42. D: The solubility curve for NaCl is nearly horizontal.
Answer choice a is the substance with the *greatest* solubility.
Answer choice b is the substance whose solubility *decreases* as temperature increases.
Answer choice c is the substance whose solubility is *most* sensitive to changes in temperature.

43. B: Significant digits indicate the precision of the measurement. Answer B has 5 significant figures. A and C each have 4. D has 3. The leading zeros in Answers A and D and are not counted as significant digits, but zeros at the end of the number (as in Answers A and B) do count. In answer D, the zero in between 2 and 9 is significant.

44. B: The Newton is defined in terms of the fundamental units meters, kilograms, and seconds (N = $kg \times m/s^2$), so it is not a fundamental unit. II is a verbal statement of $F = ma$, Newton's second law, which is true. If $F = 0$ N, then the acceleration is 0 m/s^2. If the acceleration is 0 m/s^2, then the speed · is 0 m/s or a nonzero constant. This is a nonverbal statement of Newton's first law, meaning Newton's first law can be derived from his second law. Newton's second law cannot be derived from the universal law of gravity.

45. A: The test taker who chooses a correctly combined the information in the table and recognized that the Universal Law of Gravitation is an inverse square law that relates the mass of the two bodies, the square of the distance between them, and the gravitational constant (G): $F = \frac{G(m_1 \times m_2)}{r^2}$
The test taker who chooses b used the force of Earth's gravity instead of the gravitational constant.
The test taker who chooses c inverted the masses and the distance in the formula.
The test taker who chooses d modified the gravitational constant by a factor related to Earth's gravity (i.e. divided by Earth's gravity).

46. A: The two forces described in the item stem are equal in magnitude and opposite in direction. This creates a state of equilibrium and the sphere is not moving.
The conditions necessary for the sphere to accelerate (b) are a change in direction or a change in velocity. The equal and opposite forces described in the item stem will not create either condition.
The conditions necessary for the sphere to move along a line at a 120° angle (c) are two *unequal* forces acting at 30° and 210°.
G-force is a measure of acceleration. The conditions necessary for the sphere to experience additional g-force (d) are freefall or increasing acceleration. The equal and opposite forces described in the item stem will not create either condition.

47. D: The unit for work is J or kg-m^2 / sec^2. This eliminates answer choices a, b, and c. Work = force x distance. Lifting the 1 Kg object requires a force to overcome the downward pull of gravity (1 kg x 9.81 m/sec^2 = 9.81 kg-m/sec^2). Multiplying this force by the distance of 10 meters gives 98.1 kg-m^2/s^2, or 98.1 J.

48. D: The unit of power is watts (W). The mathematical formula used to calculate power is power = work/time OR power = [(mass x gravity) x (distance)]/time. Using the values in the question, this equation gives

[(5 kg x 9.81 m/s²) x (10 m)]/5 s = 98.1 kg-m²/s³ OR 98.1 J/s OR 98.1 W.

49. B: The ideal mechanical advantage (IMA) of a simple machine ignores friction. It is the effort force divided into the resultant force. It is also the distance the effort force moves divided by the distance the resultant force moves. The IMA of a fixed pulley is 1 because all a fixed pulley does is change the direction of the effort force. A moveable pulley, however, doubles the force by increasing the distance by two. In this case, there is one fixed pulley and one floating pulley. Since the IMA of the fixed pulley is 1, and the floating pulley doubles this, the total IMA is 2.

50. B: Concerning answer A, if an object has a positive charge, it is because electrons were removed. In the case of a conductor, the electrons will migrate away from the surface, leaving a positive charge on the surface. The electric field of a negative point charge points towards the charge. The electric field of a sheet of charges will be perpendicular to the sheet.

51. B: Although Answer A is also true, Answer B correctly states the law of conservation of charge. Answer C is only partially true because there are other elementary particles with a charge. Answer D is false because a photon will produce an electron-positron pair. There is also the example of a proton and electron combining to form a neutron.

52. B: The direction of the electric field is the same as the direction of the force on a positive test charge. Moving a negative charge in the direction of the electric field requires an external force to oppose the electric field. This would increase the electron's potential energy.

53. B: An iron bar moving inside a coil of wire that contains a current would create an electromagnet. Choice a creates a magnetic field. Choice c creates an electric current. Choice d creates the Earth's magnetic field.

54. C: Wavelength determines the color of the visible light spectrum.
Sound pitch depends on the frequency (a) of the sound wave.
The loudness of a sound depends on the amplitude (b) of the sound wave.
The speed of sound (d) is a constant for any specific medium. For example, the speed of sound in air is 340 m/s.

55. C: According to the principles of constructive and destructive interference, the two wave forms shown in the item stem will create waveform c.

56. B: The wavelength is the distance (often in meters) between two peaks or two troughs of a wave. In this case, that distance is labeled as 4 meters. The height of the wave from the center is the amplitude. This wave has an amplitude of 5 meters, which is half of the total vertical distance from the top of one peak to the bottom of a trough. 2 meters represents 1/2 of the wavelength, which would be the horizontal distance across a single peak or trough, but not from peak to peak.

57. A: Polarization is a property of transverse waves when the medium vibrates in the direction perpendicular to the direction of propagation of energy. A polarizer orients these waves so they're all oscillating in the same direction. Polarization is a property of waves, not particles, so the particle nature of light cannot be used to polarize light. Nor are there tiny holes in a polarizer, although

there are thin lines. The fact that light travels in a vacuum means that light does not need a medium, but does not affect polarization. Also, light travels in transverse, not longitudinal waves.

58. B: When a tuning fork vibrates it creates areas of condensation (higher pressure) and rarefactions (lower pressure) that propagate through the air because of the air's elasticity. The distance between the condensations or rarefactions is the wavelength of the sound. The amplitude of the sound is half the difference between the pressure of the condensation and the pressure of the rarefaction. Loudness and power are both logarithmic measures that depend on the amplitude, but are not directly proportional to it. For example, doubling the amplitude will not double the loudness or power; those quantities will increase just slightly.

59. A: The frequency of a sound wave directly determines its pitch. We say the pitch of 480 Hz is higher than the pitch of 440 Hz. High and low are the words we use to describe pitch. Overtones refer to the frequencies above the fundamental frequency in a musical instrument. Two singers singing the same note at the same loudness will sound differently because their voices have different timbres.

60. C: Three full waves fit into the pipe, according to the question description. The wavelength of the third harmonic in this pipe organ is 1.2m/1.5 waves = 0.8 m. Using the wave equation ($v = \lambda f$), f = 340 m/s / 0.8 m = 425 Hz.

61. B: Bacteria and cyanobacteria have cell walls constructed from peptidoglycans – a polysaccharide and protein molecule. Other types of organisms with cell walls, for instance, plants and fungi, have cell walls composed of different polysaccharides. Plant cell walls are composed of cellulose, and fungal cell walls are composed of chitin.

62. B: Proteins in the inner membrane of the mitochondrion accept high-energy electrons from NAD and $FADH_2$, and in turn transport protons from the matrix to the intermembrane space. The high proton concentration in the intermembrane space creates a gradient which is harnessed by ATP synthase to produce ATP.

63. D: Operons are common to prokaryotes. They are units of DNA that control the transcription of DNA and code for their own regulatory proteins as well as structural proteins.

64. D: Conjugation is direct transfer of plasmid DNA between bacteria through a pilus. The F plasmid contains genes that enable bacteria to produce pili and is often the DNA that is transferred between bacteria.

65. D: The synaptonemal complex is the point of contact between homologous chromatids. It is formed when nonsister chromatids exchange genetic material through crossing over. Once meiosis I has completed, crossovers have resolved and the synaptonemal complex no longer exists. Rather, sister chromatids are held together at their centromeres prior to separation in anaphase II.

66. D: The enzyme helicase unwinds DNA. It depends on several other proteins to make the unwinding run smoothly, however. Single-strand binding protein holds the single stranded DNA in place, and topoisomerase helps relieve tension at the replication fork.

67. D: CAM photosynthesis occurs in plants that grow where water loss must be minimized, such as cacti. These plants open their stomata and fix CO_2 at night. During the day, stomata are closed, reducing water loss. Thus, photosynthesis can proceed without water loss.

68. B: DNA wrapped around histone proteins is called chromatin. In a eukaryotic cell, DNA is always associated with protein; it is not "naked" as with prokaryotic cells.

69. D: Each time a cell divides; a few base pairs of DNA at the end of each chromosome are lost. Telomerase is an enzyme that uses a built-in template to add a short sequence of DNA over and over at the end of chromosomes—a sort of protective "cap". This prevents the loss of genetic material with each round of DNA replication.

70. A: DNA synthesis on the lagging strand forms short segments called Okazaki fragments. Because DNA polymerase can only add nucleotides in the $5' \rightarrow 3'$ direction, lagging strand synthesis is discontinuous. The final product is formed when DNA ligase joins Okazaki fragments together.

71. C: Insertions and deletions cause frameshift mutations. These mutations cause all subsequent nucleotides to be displaced by one position, and thereby cause all the amino acids to be different than they would have been if the mutation had not occurred.

72. A: Transcription is the process of creating an RNA strand from a DNA template. All forms of RNA, for example mRNA, tRNA, and rRNA, are products of transcription.

73. B: In ferns, the mature diploid plant is called a sporophyte. Sporophytes undergo meiosis to produce spores, which develop into gametophytes, which produce gametes.

74. C: Hybridization between two different species would result in more genetic variation than sexual reproduction within a species.

75. B: Phyletic gradualism is the view that evolution occurs at a more or less constant rate. Contrary to this view, punctuated equilibrium holds that evolutionary history consists of long periods of stasis punctuated by geologically short periods of evolution. This theory predicts that there will be few fossils revealing intermediate stages of evolution, whereas phyletic gradualism views the lack of intermediate-stage fossils as a deficit in the fossil record that will resolve when enough specimens are collected.

76. B: Adaptive radiation is the evolution of several species from a single ancestor. It occurs when a species colonizes a new area and members diverge geographically as they adapt to somewhat different conditions.

77. A: Vultures eat carrion, or dead animals, so they are considered scavengers. Detritivores are heterotrophs that eat decomposing organic matter such as leaf litter. They are usually small.

78. D: Stomata are openings on leaves that allow for gas exchange, which is essential for photosynthesis. Stomata are formed by guard cells, which open and close based on their turgidity.

79. A: Monocots differ from dicots in that they have one cotyledon, or embryonic leaf in their embryos. They also have parallel veination, fibrous roots, petals in multiples of three, and a random arrangement of vascular bundles in their stems.

80. B: Platelets are cell fragments that are involved in blood clotting. Platelets are the site for the blood coagulation cascade. Its final steps are the formation of fibrinogen which, when cleaved, forms fibrin, the "skeleton" of the blood clot.

81. A: The large intestine's main function is the reabsorption of water into the body to form solid waste. It also allows for the absorption of vitamin K produced by microbes living inside the large intestine.

82. B: Secondary succession occurs when a habitat has been entirely or partially disturbed or destroyed by abandonment, burning, storms, etc.

83. B: Epiphytes are plants that grow in the canopy of trees, and the tropical rain forest has a rich canopy because of its density and extensive moisture.

84. D: Within a habitat, there is a maximum number of individuals that can continue to thrive, known as the habitat's carrying capacity. When the population size approaches this number, population growth will stop.

85. B: A mineral's true color is observed by conducting a streak test on unglazed porcelain tile. Paper is not appropriate for a streak test because it does not have the correct physical properties. External observation (inspecting the mineral's outer surface) is not sufficient to establish true color since streak tests sometimes reveal a color that is different from the substance's external hue. Finally, the luster test is not used to determine color.

86. D: Galena, pyrite, and magnetite are examples of minerals with a metallic luster. Opal is an example of a mineral with a greasy luster, and diamonds have an adamantine luster. Muscovite and stilbite are examples of minerals with a pearly luster. Other types of luster include dull, silky, waxy, and sub-metallic.

87. B: According to the Dana classification system, gold, silver, and copper belong to the elemental class. Members of the oxide class include chromite and magnetite, and hydrocarbons and acetates are members of the organic class. Sulfide minerals include pyrite and galena.

88. A: According to the Dana system, minerals that contain the anion SO_4^{2-} are part of the sulfate class. Sulfate minerals are typically formed in environments where highly saline water evaporates. Gypsum is an example of a mineral that belongs to the sulfate class.

89. C: Minerals that form on the sea floor from discarded shells are most likely part of the carbonate class. Minerals that form in karst regions and evaporitic settings may also be carbonates. Examples of minerals in the carbonate class include aragonite, dolomite, calcite, and siderite.

90. C: When salt water penetrates fractures in rocks and leaves behind salt crystals that cause the rock to fracture, it is considered physical rather than chemical weathering. Chemical weathering involves changes in the molecules that comprise the rocks, while physical weathering occurs when external factors act on the rock without changing its chemical composition in any way.

91. D: Weathering causes erosion, which often leads to transportation and the deposition of eroded material. After the eroded material is deposited in a new location, lithification proceeds and the sedimentary cycle begins anew.

92. A: Non-detrital sedimentary rock is produced by chemical precipitation. In contrast, detrital sedimentary rocks are comprised of pre-existing rocks, such as quartz, or weathered products of pre-existing rocks, such as clay.

93. B: Rocks such as olivine that are found at the top of Bowen's reaction series weather more quickly than rocks found lower in the series. This is because rocks high in the series crystallize at higher temperatures than those found lower in the series. This means they are less stable and more susceptible to weathering than rocks that crystallize at lower temperatures, such as quartz.

94. B: Since the mountain in Figure 1 has the oldest rock in its core and the youngest rock in its outer layers, it is best described as an anticline. Any mountain that results from a crustal fold and has an upward, convex shape is called an antiform. Mountains in which the rocks are progressively older from the outer layers to the core are anticlines. Synclines have downward, or concave, folds, and fault-block mountains result when faults in continental crust cause certain sections to lift or tilt. Grabens are a formation associated with fault-block mountains.

95. C: When fault-block mountains such as those in the Western United States are formed, sections that are lifted by tensional forces are called horsts. Blocks that are lowered in elevation are called grabens. The term "rift" refers to the entire area that is affected by the separation of a continental plate.

96. C: When water changes directly from a solid to a gas, skipping the liquid state, it is known as sublimation. It typically occurs when snow or ice is exposed to direct sunlight, and it is possible at unusually low atmospheric pressure points.

97. D: The Cretaceous-Tertiary event, during which non-avian dinosaurs became extinct, occurred approximately 65.5 million years ago during the Mesozoic era. It is the most recent of the five major extinction events that have occurred throughout the Earth's history.

98. A: The appearance of the Coriolis effect in the Earth's oceans is caused by the Earth's rotation. The Coriolis effect results when free objects such as water move over a rotating surface such as the Earth. As water moves from the poles towards the Equator, it curves slightly westward, while water moving in the opposite direction (from the Equator towards the poles) moves slightly eastward.

99. C: Thermohaline circulation is caused by variations in seawater density caused by both temperature and salinity differences. This process, which affects subsurface ocean currents, contributes to the mixing of seawater and accounts for the relative uniformity of the water's physical and chemical properties.

100. C: When cold, nutrient-rich water is allowed to rise to the surface because winds parallel to a landmass's coast blow the surface water towards the open sea, it is called upwelling. Upwelling brings the remains of dead sea creatures to the surface, providing food for phytoplankton. Zooplanktons consume the phytoplankton, and larger organisms consume the zooplanktons. Thus, upwelling allows marine life to thrive near coastal areas.

101. D: The frequency of ocean waves is measured by the number of wave crests that pass a given point each second. The crest of a wave is its highest point, and the trough is its lowest point. The distance between two subsequent crests is called wavelength, and the height is the distance between a single wave's trough and crest.

102. C: The majority of the solar energy that reaches Earth is absorbed by the oceans, which make up 71 percent of the Earth's surface. Because of water's high specific heat capacity, oceans can absorb and store large quantities of heat, thus preventing drastic increases in the overall atmospheric temperature.

103. A: Air is a mixture composed of elements (e.g. nitrogen and oxygen) and compounds (e.g. CO_2). It is homogenous since the distribution of the constituent molecules is the same throughout the mixture.

104. C: Tropical climate zones are characterized by frequent rainfall, especially during the monsoon season, and by moderate temperatures that vary little from season to season or between night and day. Tropical zones do experience frequent rainfall, which leads to abundant vegetation.

105. D: The asteroid belt in our solar system is located between Mars and Jupiter. The asteroid belt is populated by asteroids and dwarf planets that are distributed thinly enough that spacecraft can pass though the belt with relative ease.

106. A: The distance from the Earth to the Sun is equal to one astronomical unit. An astronomical unit (AU) is equal to 93 million miles, and is far smaller than a light year or a parsec. A light year is defined as the distance light can travel in a vacuum in one year, and is equal to roughly 64,341 AU. A parsec is the parallax of one arcsecond, and is equal to 206.26×10^3 astronomical units.

107. D: The physical structure of the universe is thought to consist of filaments (walls of superclusters, clusters, and galaxies) that surround large, bubble-like voids. Filaments are the largest structures in the universe, with some forming huge structures like the Great Wall and the Sloan Great Wall.

108. A: The Hertzsprung-Russell (H-R) Diagram is used primarily to determine a star's age by comparing its temperature and luminosity. These two variables are plotted, and a given star's values can be compared to those of other stars to estimate its age and evolutionary stage. Stars on the Main Sequence of the diagram have roughly proportional luminosity and temperature values, while white dwarf stars have low luminosity relative to their temperature. Some giant stars have low temperatures relative to their luminosity.

109. A: Pioneer species colonize vacant habitats, and the first such species in a habitat demonstrate primary succession. Succession on rock or lava often begins with lichens. Lichens need very little organic material and can erode rock into soil to provide a growth substrate for other organisms.

110. A: Transportation by humans or human-associated means is not considered a natural dispersal process.

111. D: Genetic engineering is a general term to describe altering DNA sequences through adding or removing pieces of DNA from a native sequence. Restriction enzymes perform this "clipping" function.

112. C: Day-neutral plants are not affected by day length in their flowering times. Rather, they respond to other environmental cues like temperature and water.

113. D: Mercury is a fat-soluble pollutant and can be stored in body tissues. Animals higher up the food chain that eat other animals are most likely to accumulate mercury in their bodies.

114. B: The U.S. Army Corps of Engineers is a decentralized organization responsible for protecting navigation on the nation's waterways. The corps tries to keep controls, permits, and required paperwork to a minimum. They believe an applicant requesting a permit should receive a quick response. They are responsible for specific activities in U.S. waters including:
  * Dams and dikes
  * Excavation, dredging, and disposal activities
  * Construction of artificial islands and installations on the continental shelf
  * Dumping of dredged material into U.S. waterways
  * Transporting dredged material for disposal in the oceans
  * Issuing permits for some waterway-related activities

115. D: Environmental science is the interdisciplinary study of the interactions of the physical, chemical, and biological parts of all living and nonliving things that occur naturally on earth. Sometimes referred to as the "natural environment" (as opposed to the human-influenced "built environment"), components include plants, animals, microorganisms, rocks, air, water, climate, energy, radiation, electric charge, and magnetism-in other words, anything that is not man-made or created from or a by-product of human activity.

Environmental scientists study and monitor the quality of the natural environment, try to interpret the current impact and predict the future impact of human activity. They then develop sensible strategies and potential solutions to prevent and/or restore damaged ecosystems. They work with architects and engineers to plan buildings, highways, and utility projects that protect water resources and do as little damage as possible to the affected land. They are concerned with climate change, conservation, biodiversity, groundwater and soil contamination, air and noise pollution, and waste management. Because they deal with man-made issues, they must also have knowledge of economics, the law, and the social sciences.

116. A: The Food and Drug Administration (FDA) is an agency within the U.S. Department of Health and Human Services. Its purpose is to ensure the safety, effectiveness, manufacturing, packaging, and labeling of food, medical, and cosmetic products used and/or consumed by humans, as well as food additives and drugs given to animals. The FDA has the power and authority to approve, ban, and control the marketing and distribution of these products. The agency charges fees to the manufacturers who have applied for approval. In return, the FDA is required to meet specific "performance benchmarks" during the approval process.

The FDA doesn't actually test products; that is the manufacturer's responsibility. The FDA reviews and verifies study data provided by the product's sponsor. FDA doctors, statisticians, chemists, pharmacologists, and scientists review the data from clinical trials, manufacturing specifications, drug stability, and labeling and packaging designs. The agency accepts and approves the product (benefits outweigh risks), declares it "approvable" (minor problems need to be addressed before final approval), or declares the product "not approvable" because of concerns about the safety and/or effectiveness of the product.

117. B: Self-explanatory.

118. C: It is entirely possible that the molecules of the compound can decompose at the elevated temperatures before the boiling point of the material is attained. Reducing the pressure lowers the

temperature at which materials boil, so distillation can occur before the material ever becomes hot enough to decompose.

High-boiling materials do boil at normal pressure, but at temperatures that are high enough to be a concern in regard to safety, energy use, etc.

Boiling point and vapor pressure are inversely related; higher vapor pressure means lower boiling point.

The melting point of a compound is not related to its boiling point.

119. C: Activated charcoal powder acts as an adsorbent. The molecules of colored impurities tend to be polar compounds that adhere to the surfaces of the charcoal powder. Subsequently, filtration to remove the charcoal powder also removes the colored impurities.

Filtration alone can only remove impurities that are present as solids, colored or otherwise.

A cosolvent is used in recrystallization either to form a suitable solvent system or to initiate the formation of crystals.

Chromatography is a procedure for separating compounds in a mixture and is not part of the recrystallization process.

120. C: In all forms of chromatography, the separation of components in a mixture is achieved by the differential rates at which the compounds adsorb and desorb from the surfaces of the stationary phase particles. The more times this can happen as the mixture progresses down the column, the better the separation of the components.

Solubility plays a role in chromatography but does not solely determine the separation of the components.

Similarly, polarity plays a role in chromatography but does not solely determine the separation of components.

Absorption is a different process than adsorption and is not involved in chromatography.